THE OFFICIAL
ILLUSTRATED HISTORY

Carlton Books Limited
Part of Welbeck Non-Fiction Ltd
20 Mortimer Street
London W1T 3JW

ISBN: 978-1-78739-335-6 (Trade Edition)
ISBN: 978-1-78739-400-1 (Special Edition)

Project Manager: Martin Corteel
Editor: Ross Hamilton
Assistant Editor: David Ballheimer
Design: James Pople
Art Direction: Luke Griffin
Picture Research: Paul Langan
Production: Rachel Burgess

Printed in Italy

THE OFFICIAL
ILLUSTRATED HISTORY

DAVID CLAYTON

Foreword by
PEP GUARDIOLA

CARLTON
BOOKS

CONTENTS

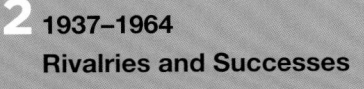

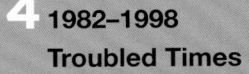

FOREWORD

The 2019/20 season marks the 125th anniversary of our Club.

To be the manager during such an important milestone is a genuine honour for me. As you know, I have a great interest in history, and I learn something new every day about our Club.

Manchester City: The Official Illustrated History has everything you need to know about our past. It is so important to immerse yourself in what makes a football club what it is, and it makes you feel privileged to be able to create new history.

It's quite something that our Club became Manchester City in 1894. My old club, Barcelona, started life in 1899 and, a year later, another of my former clubs, Bayern Munich were first formed, so it was clearly an amazing time in the history of football.

In this book, you will learn about the players, managers and moments that made Manchester City what it is today. It wasn't always great – we've had our hard times and waited many years to win a trophy. The drought was 35 years before we won the FA Cup in 2011, and there were 44 years between our second and third league titles.

But the one thing that impresses me the most is the loyalty of our supporters. They have always been there and to learn that we had crowds of 60,000, 70,000 or even more than 80,000 in the 1930s on a regular basis is amazing. Good or bad, throughout these first 125 years, our fans have always been there in their thousands.

We know that the team of today is creating a new history. We've broken records, won trophies and we aim to continue creating new history that can make our fans proud for as long as we can.

Then, maybe in 25, 50 or even 100 years, they will look back on this period and say, "Those guys were good!" I hope so, because that is why we do what we do.

I hope I can play even a small part in the history of Manchester City. This is an amazing club and there are more chapters to write…

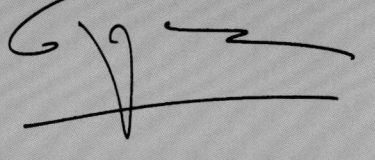

Pep Guardiola, July 2019

Left: Pep Guardiola has overseen the most successful period in Manchester City history since he arrived in 2016.

Beer at its Best TETI
MPLEMAN

FOURMIDABLES
18/19
COMMUNITY SHIELD WINNERS
CARABAO CUP WINNERS
PREMIER LEAGUE CHAMPIONS
FA CUP WINNERS

INTRODUCTION

Manchester City Football Club has a rich and vibrant history – that is a fact nobody can deny.

Celebrating 125 years since the club officially came into existence in April 1894, *The Official Illustrated History* travels from the beginning to the present day, charting City's many highs and lows and telling the story through images and words.

It's a journey that travels from humble beginnings right through to the history-making team assembled by Pep Guardiola – already the club's most successful manager just three years into his tenure.

Each season is covered with the back story of the managers and players who first put City on the map, with some incredible stories and events along the way.

From the Welsh wizardry of Billy Meredith to the goal machine that is Sergio Agüero; from the fearless goalkeeping of Bert Trautmann through to the technically brilliant Ederson Moraes; from the leadership skills of Roy Paul through to the club's greatest and most successful skipper, Vincent Kompany; from the elegance of Neil Young to the genius of David Silva – the tales of the players are vividly told in a series of legends' profiles and shown during the Blues' rollercoaster history of leaps and pitfalls.

Then there are the managers: the pioneers, the innovators, the thinkers and the serial trophy winners.

Moments in time, captured by the camera lens that often need no words, and images that encapsulate historic events preserved for eternity.

And then there are the City fans!

The people who have loyally stood by the club through thick and thin – and sometimes even thinner – and turned out in their thousands throughout, from the moments when Maine Road was bursting at the seams with crowds that have still never been matched outside of London, to the dark days of third-tier football… City fans have seen it all and have been there, done that. Still they come to support their heroes in their thousands, no matter what.

The Official Illustrated History will take you from the start of the adventure to the present day, celebrating the moments that have made Manchester City FC unique in so many ways.

Some of the stories defy logic, others will make you smile, and there might even be moments when your eyes well with nostalgia of a bygone era.

But one thing is for certain: nothing about this football club is ever dull.

So fasten your seatbelts and prepare to travel through time.

City fans may sing, "We're not really here," but you are about to see that they've always been there and you're about to understand the reasons why.

Enjoy the ride!

Left top: Manager Joe Mercer and his Division One title-winners parade the Football League Championship trophy at Maine Road before a friendly with Bury in May 1968.

Left: Pep Guardiola and the "Fourmidables" celebrate their unprecedented domestic sweep of all available English trophies during the 2018/19 campaign with a parade in the centre of Manchester.

1. 1880–1937: ORIGINS AND RAPID PROGRESS

The formation of the club that eventually became Manchester City FC can be traced back to 1880, with Reverend Arthur Connell and church wardens William Beastow and Thomas Goodbehere – along with Connell's daughter Anna - all playing integral roles in creating a sporting distraction for the lost youth of East Manchester.

Founded as a salvation for disaffected local youths, in many ways, the creation of a local football team created a healthy distraction from deeply troubled times on the often violent streets of Manchester and the Gorton area in particular where gang violence, poverty and alcoholism were rife.

St Mark's (West Gorton) largely followed in the footsteps of a cricket team formed a few years before that had proved popular in the summer months. The newly-formed football club would provide an interest during the dark, damp Manchester winters and quickly gathered momentum.

In late 1880, St Mark's played their first recorded game against a Baptist team from Macclesfield, losing 2-1. The fledgling club were part of the inaugural Division Two of 1892/93 and finished fifth in the first campaign. With no real home to call their own, the Club's pioneers played their first home matches in and around a small radius in East Manchester. Clowes Street, Kirkmanshulme Lane Cricket Club, Queens Road, Pink Bank Lane and Reddish Lane – all within a couple of miles of each other at best.

There would be several name changes, too, including West Gorton, Gorton AFC and Ardwick FC and it was during the lifespan of Ardwick that a more permanent home was needed to accommodate the growing crowds attending matches. Hyde Road was the Club's first purpose-built enclosed home ground in 1887. Hemmed in by a railway track to the west and sidings north – train drivers would often slow down to catch a glimpse of the football being played! The ground was very basic, had one stand and no changing facilities, with players forced to get changed at the nearby Hyde Road Hotel, though gradually, the ground was developed piece by piece.

However, all was not well off the pitch. Ardwick were effectively no longer able to continue operating due to various financial issues and after lengthy meetings and much discussion among local officials, they played their final game – a 5-2 loss to Walsall Swifts in early April 1894. Shortly after, and with the community of East Manchester pledging to pull together for the good of the city and the legacy of Ardwick, Manchester City Football Club Limited were officially formed and recognized by Companies House on 16 April 1894.

On 1 September 1894, Manchester City played their first official league game against Bury, losing 4-2 and the first victory would come just a week later with a 4-1 win over Burslem Port Vale, watched by an estimated crowd of 4,000 at Hyde Road, where Ardwick had called home since 1887.

City's first major signing as such would be inspired. Promising winger Billy Meredith from tiny North Wales outfit Chirk agreed to join the newly formed club and would go on to become one of City's all-time greats. The "Welsh Wizard" would play 393 games for the Blues over two spells, scoring 151 goals and becoming the superstar of his day.

The first flush of success for City was confirmed on 22 April 1899 when a 4-1 win over Blackpool completed the 1898/99 campaign in style with the Blues crowned champions and promoted to Division One for the very first time. A top-flight side at last, City finished a respectable seventh in their first Division One campaign, but would be relegated after just three seasons in the top flight at the end of the 1901/02 campaign following a dreadful run of just three wins from the opening 20 matches – and

Previous pages: Maine Road is packed for an FA Cup tie against Portsmouth in January 1936. Eric Brook netted a hat-trick as City won 3-0 in front of 53,340 fans.

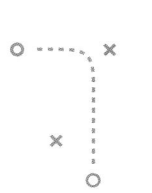

Left: Legendary captain Sam Cowan holds the FA Cup aloft as City enjoy a bus-top parade through the streets of Manchester after the 2-1 defeat of Portsmouth in the 1934 final. It was the Blues' second FA Cup win.

despite a much stronger end to the campaign that saw eight wins and three draws from the last 16 matches, the Blues finished bottom.

It wasn't only Christmas that the people of Manchester celebrated on 25 December 1902. The inaugural Manchester derby took place in front of an estimated 40,000 as Manchester United held Manchester City to a 1-1 draw. The teams had met many times in various guises over the years, but Newton Heath didn't become Manchester United until 1902 so this was the first time the teams had met as City and United, and the rivalry was truly up and running. The festive clash of the Manchester clans took place at United's Bank Street in Clayton – less than a mile away from the future site of City's current home, the Etihad Stadium.

Joshua Parlby, Sam Ormerod and Tom Maley had been City's early managers and it was Maley who guided City back to the top flight as the Blues clinched the Division Two title in style, scoring 95 goals in 34 games and taking the crown for the second time in four years. The 1903/04 campaign proved to be a case of so close, yet so far. Maley's City dropped three points in the final three games and missed out on a first top-division title to Sheffield club The Wednesday, though a packed schedule of matches towards the end, including four matches in a week, hardly helped the Blues' cause.

The disappointment would be short-lived, however, as on 23 April 1904, City finally made their mark in English football. Playing at Crystal Palace in London, the Blues took on Bolton Wanderers in front of an FA Cup final crowd of 61,374. City had seen off Sunderland, Woolwich Arsenal, Middlesbrough and title rivals The Wednesday to reach the final and were determined to return north with the trophy. Backed by thousands of travelling City fans – many of whom slept overnight at various London railway stations – skipper Billy Meredith scored the only goal, 23 minutes in, to deservedly secure the club's biggest success yet.

Despite the success, the season that followed would prove something of a disaster for City. The Blues were in the title race for most of the campaign when an alleged bribery scandal surfaced with devastating effects. Worse still, at the centre of the controversy was star winger Billy Meredith – the club's inspirational driving force and crowd hero – who stood accused of attempting to bribe an Aston Villa player to let City win the final game of the season. As a result of an investigation, the Football Association (FA) suspended Meredith for one year, during which time City refused to pay his wages. This, in turn, led to counterclaims from the Welsh winger that City paid players more than the fixed-wage ceiling, and manager Tom Maley would later be banned from football for life as a result. It was a toxic situation and Meredith felt he had been made a scapegoat, suggesting it was something Maley had asked him to do.

Maley's, Meredith's and City's reputations were in tatters and the team that had just been maturing into a genuine force was, as a result, ripped apart.

Worse still, before the end of his 12-month ban, Meredith signed for Manchester United along with City stars Sandy Turnbull, Herbert Burgess and Jimmy Bannister and, although new manager Harry Newbould began to fashion a side from the players that remained, a grimly determined Meredith helped United become the first Manchester club to win the top-flight title after just two seasons with the Reds.

City found it difficult to recover and were relegated in 1909/10, but bounced back immediately the season after when, following an unbelievably close finish, the Blues pipped Oldham Athletic, Hull City and Derby County by a single point to clinch the second-tier title.

City plodded on after returning to Division One without finishing higher than fifth until the First World War broke out in 1914, lasting for more than four years, with football reduced to regional leagues as players left to serve their country.

Left: Manchester City squad photo after the 1904 FA Cup triumph – note Billy Meredith, middle row, first left.

Frank Hesham became the first City player to be killed in action and the Blues lost several more team members – past and present – as the conflict continued. Ex-City star Sandy Turnbull was killed in action and the Blues' home ground, Hyde Road, was used as a giant stable and grazing area for horses after being commandeered by the War Department.

After the conflict ended and the Football League resumed, City and the rest of world football tried to resume some sort of normality. On 27 March 1920, King George V attended City's 2-1 home win over Liverpool at Hyde Road, with Horace Barnes' brace suitably impressing the royal visitor. It was the first occasion a reigning monarch had been present at a game outside of London but, eight months later, tragedy struck and pointed City's fate in a different direction.

A catastrophic blaze at Hyde Road completely gutted the Main Stand, leaving nothing other than charred wood on the mud embankment. Though some reports in later years claimed it was an accident associated with Guy Fawkes Night, club ledgers and paperwork suggest it occurred on 10 November. Documentation and records dating back more than 20 years were lost forever in the fire and the club's faithful hound, Nell, also perished in the flames. Given the intensity of the blaze, it is perhaps a minor miracle that no other lives were lost. The cause was believed to be a stray cigarette butt, rather than a spark from a bonfire or a firework.

Despite the setback, City's 1-1 draw away to Newcastle United completed a fine season. Tommy Browell's goal earned a point as the Blues finished runners-up in Division One to Burnley in their continued pursuit of an elusive first top-flight title.

There were more than a few eyebrows raised when, in 1921, City re-signed Billy Meredith on a free transfer, not least because the veteran winger was then 47 years old. Time had healed some old wounds and, despite his 15-year stint with United, many City fans still felt he was coming back to the club he'd never wanted to leave – and when he helped the Blues beat United 4-1 during the 1921/22 campaign, he was fully forgiven for his defection!

Former Manchester United manager Ernest Mangnall had been in the City hot-seat since 1912 and, having been a driving force of the Reds' move into their new Old Trafford stadium during his reign, he knew City also had to find a grand new home in order to remain competitive. Thus, Mangnall would, once again, play a huge part in a Manchester giant finding a new home. On 28 April 1922, after more than 35 years of residence, City played their final game at Hyde Road – a 0-0 draw with Newcastle United.

Having been the best-supported club in Manchester for a number of years, the Blues had outgrown the ground and could no longer remain at Hyde Road while United played at the 80,000-capacity Old Trafford. The Blues' home was dilapidated and in need of a major overhaul, so the decision was taken to find a new, state-of-the-art stadium and, in 1923, that became a reality. On 25 August that year, City played their first home game at their new Maine Road installations.

Dubbed the "Wembley of the North", Maine Road was constructed in the heart of Manchester's Moss Side district on an area of land adjacent to Dog Kennel Lane with a capacity of more than 80,000 and was designed by renowned architect Charles Swain at a total construction cost of approximately

£100,000. The Blues' first home game was against Sheffield United. Horace Barnes became the first player to score at Maine Road, with a 68th-minute goal, and 3 minutes later, Tom Johnson doubled the Blues' lead. City won 2-1 and were watched by a crowd of 56,993. Home sweet home, indeed.

Relocating to Moss Side coincided with a boom time for the club, with some huge attendances at Maine Road as fans warmed to the new home. A fourth-round FA Cup tie against Cardiff attracted a record crowd in excess of 76,000 fans and the Blues went on to reach the semi-final before losing out to Newcastle United. The cup run apart, it was a pretty average campaign for Mangnall's side who, despite having a new base, finished in 11th place in Division One. Mangnall, who had managed City for 12 years, stood down after the season ended, his place in the history of Manchester football secured.

The 1924/25 season began with new manager David Ashworth at the helm. The former Oldham manager had steered Liverpool to the title two years earlier and he jumped at the chance of becoming City boss when the offer arrived. City finished 10th in his first campaign and were steady but unspectacular throughout. Ashworth's second season in charge would be anything but dull, however. He oversaw the first ever Maine Road Manchester derby, which ended 1-1, Sam Cowan scoring the Blues' goal with just shy of 63,000 people watching.

Thereafter, a bizarre set of results followed, leading to Ashworth resigning from his post. City had a 1-1, 2-2, 3-3 and even a 4-4 draw in the space of six games before thrashing Burnley 8-3. Two days after beating the Clarets, City lost by the same score – 8-3 – away to Sheffield United. The Blues then lost the next 4 matches, shipping another 17 goals, and Ashworth jumped before he was shoved. A committee, which included Albert Alexander and several directors, took on the day-to-day running

of the team while a replacement was sought.

The FA Cup brought much needed relief for the 1925/26 season, with City going all the way to a first Wembley appearance and a game against Bolton Wanderers. Along the way there was an incredible tie against Crystal Palace, with the Blues triumphing 11-4.

However, City's first Wembley Stadium match in 1926 for the FA Cup final proved to be a day of revenge for Bolton Wanderers – beaten in the 1904 FA Cup final by the Blues – who triumphed 1-0 in front of 91,347 fans. It was the biggest crowd City had played in front of up to that point.

New boss Peter Hodge took the reins for the last couple of games but City lost their top-flight status, finishing second to bottom. Hodge almost guided the club to promotion on the first attempt in 1926/27, but the Blues finished in third place in the cruellest of circumstances. City and Portsmouth were level on points going into the final game, with both sides winning their matches, but despite an emphatic 8-0 win over relegated Bradford City on the final day, Portsmouth's 5-1 win over Preston North End meant it was the south-coast club who went up, by virtue of the merest fraction on goal average, in what was to be the tightest promotion race ever, leaving City to face another season in Division Two. In Hodge, though, the club had an excellent manager and, in 1927/28, the pain of the previous campaign was forgotten as the club went up as champions, averaging 38,000 at Maine Road – the highest average gate anywhere in the country. Hodge had brought in Barnsley forwards Fred Tilson and Eric Brook for a combined fee of £6,000 toward the end of the season and both men would play integral parts in the club's future.

Season 1928/29 was all about consolidation, and the finish of eighth place was satisfying for all concerned, but particularly for crowd idol Tommy Johnson, who scored 38 goals in 40 league games – a record that still stands today.

Above: : A 19-year-old Frank Swift clears the danger as Portsmouth attack during the 1934 FA Cup Final at Wembley. City go on to win 2-1.

A young Matt Busby made his debut for City the following season (1929/30) as Hodge's men chased a historic league and cup double. Impressively, the Blues eventually finished third, though were some 13 points adrift of the champions, Sheffield Wednesday, while losing out to Hull City in the FA Cup fifth round. A 10-1 home victory over Swindon Town and a 6-1 win at Liverpool were the highlights of the campaign but Hodge's decision to sell Johnson to Everton was greeted with disbelief by his army of fans at Maine Road. The "Toffees" had obviously not forgotten Johnson's heroics during the previous season when he bagged five of City's goals in a 6-2 win at the then champions' own ground!

Hodge came in for his first real taste of criticism as the Blues' boss when goals were hard to come by for the 1930/31 campaign. Brook ended top scorer with 16 but strike partner Tilson was injured for much of the campaign and Johnson's replacement, Tommy Tait, had left for Bolton Wanderers. David Halliday had been signed from Arsenal and added another 14 goals but the momentum had been lost somewhere along the line.

The next season brought even less cheer and, although the Maine Road crowds were still huge and Hodge managed to field the same side for most of the campaign, the Blues finished in a disappointing

14th place, though a decent FA Cup run was only ended by the mighty Arsenal, who beat the Blues 1-0 at Villa Park in the semi-final. Halliday top-scored with a total of 32 goals in all competitions but the Tommy Johnson saga was still to take one more twist.

Peter Hodge left Maine Road in 1932 to return to one of his former clubs, Leicester City. He had taken City as far as he could and Wilf Wild was promoted to look after first-team affairs, somewhat reluctantly. His first season in charge was memorable in many ways – though not in the league, where City would slump to 16th – but the FA Cup campaign proved to be an entirely different story. Gateshead, Walsall, Bolton, Burnley and Derby were dispatched en route to Wembley to face Everton and former City idol Tommy Johnson. If that wasn't enough, the legendary Dixie Dean led the line for the Merseyside giants. It was quite a combination for the Merseysiders, and they triumphed 3-0 on the day.

City's 29-year wait for silverware continued, though City skipper Sam Cowan vowed to return the following year and lift the trophy for the Blues. Few thought it was anything other than optimistic bluster considering the club's fortunes in the league, but Cowan was determined to make his prophecy come true.

Above: The City team which played and lost 1-0 to Bolton Wanderers in the 1926 FA Cup final, City's first appearance at Wembley stadium. Left to right: Sam Cookson, Tommy Johnson, Charlie Pringle, Frank Roberts, Tommy Browell, Jim Goodchild, Billy Austin, George Hicks, Jimmy McMullan, Phil McCloy and Sam Cowen.

The 1933/34 season saw Wild's men improve in the league and again thrive in the FA Cup – a competition the Blues were rapidly making their own. In the league, things were steady up until two days before Christmas when Wolves ruined many a Blues fan's festivities by beating City 8-0 at Molineux. Wild decided to give young goalkeeper Frank Swift his debut two days later, but it was to be an unhappy start to his career, as Derby County beat City 4-1 on Christmas Day. If the youngster feared for his place, he must have been terrified a week later when West Brom thrashed the Blues 7-2 at Maine Road. A turkey of a festive period if ever there was one. It was a sticky period for the club but, 12 days later, the FA Cup tie with Blackburn offered the opportunity for some New Year optimism. Driven on by skipper Cowan, City won 3-1 and then saw off Hull and Sheffield Wednesday in rounds four and five – both after away draws – before taking on Stoke City at Maine Road.

It was a game that would be etched into the record books as 84,569 fans crammed into the Blues' home ground to see the game. Stoke had a young Stanley Matthews on their team but it was Eric Brook who won the day for the Blues, scoring the only goal of the game with his cross looping over the visitors' keeper for the winner. Then it was on to the semi-final for a third successive year to face cup favourites Aston Villa. Three goals in five incredible first-half minutes all but settled the tie by the break, with City going in 4-0 up. Fred Tilson bagged four on the day as City eventually routed Villa 6-1. Cowan had instilled a belief and determination to right a wrong, and the final would present the chance to avenge Portsmouth, who had pipped them to promotion by the slenderest of margins seven years earlier. It was an opportunity too good to miss

Playing in front of a crowd of 93,258, Pompey employed rough-house tactics to try to shake a confident City out of their stride, with Tilson and Herd the targets of some nasty challenges, and it was Portsmouth who led 1-0 at the interval. Cowan roared at his team-mates to show the spirit needed to become champions and it worked wonders as the brilliant Tilson scored two late second-half goals (minutes 74 and 88) to win the game and the FA Cup for City 2-1. Sam Cowan, just as he'd predicted 12 months earlier, lifted the trophy to the jubilant hordes from Manchester.

The 1934/35 season began well for Wilf Wild's side, with just one defeat in the opening nine league games. The FA Cup holders were showing the confidence of a side that believed they could, at last, make a serious challenge for the Division One title.

Defender Sam Barkas had joined the club from Bradford for £5,000 the previous April and the stylish left-back, coupled with the excellent Bill Dale at right-back, gave the Blues a nice balance at the rear.

Tilson, Herd and Brook were once again scoring freely and, for a time, it looked like the Blues could possibly win their first ever top-flight championship. Somewhere along the line, though, City lost the thread, with a four-game New Year goal drought ringing alarm bells. In April, Matt Busby left Maine Road to join Liverpool after eight years with the Blues. Any hopes City had of the title faded on the season run-in, where just one win in nine represented a blip at the worst possible time. City managed to finish a respectable fourth, but it was still a disappointment, and the 10-point gap to champions Arsenal had fans wondering about what might have been.

The Club had been in existence as Manchester City for 41 years but still the wait for a title went on. Not for too much longer, however. Five victories from the opening six fixtures of the 1935/36 season raised expectation levels among the City fans but, once again, Wild's team flattered to deceive and won just four of the next 17 league games. Wild decided the team needed a new direction and inspiration. Blackpool star Peter Doherty was attracting attention from a whole host of clubs,

Above: The talented Peter Doherty in action for City away to Fulham in February 1939.

but it was City boss Wild who made a firm cash offer – a club-record £10,000 – which the Seasiders reluctantly accepted.

Almost 40,000 turned up for his debut against Preston North End at Maine Road, but the visitors spoiled the party, winning 3-1. Doherty had impressed sufficiently but there was much more to come from this supremely talented Irishman.

He helped inspire a 6-0 win over Middlesbrough and the 7-0 demolition of Bolton Wanderers before the season ended and, with only nine games played, he was making the transfer fee look like peanuts. City finished 9th but Wilf Wild, Peter Doherty and Manchester City's greatest moment was less than 12 months away…

The 1936/37 season began with a 2-0 away defeat to Middlesbrough and there was little to suggest that Wild's fifth successive campaign in charge of the Blues would be anything special.

Ten goals, however, in the next games – both at Maine Road – showed that gifted forward Peter Doherty's influence was beginning to spread throughout the team. The 4-0 win over Leeds United and the 6-2 demolition of West Brom had the home fans drooling for more. Could Doherty prove to be the final piece of the Wild jigsaw? The following games suggested otherwise as City won just one of their next 11 matches – the Blues were living up to their nickname of "the Great Unpredictables", blowing hot and cold without warning. In fact, 12 points from a possible 28 was more like relegation form and it could be argued that, in today's "success yesterday" culture, even the highly respected Wild may well have been shown the door at Maine Road.

Patience – an unusual and rarely used word in the modern game – was to pay off for the City board and, in mid-November, the Blues finally began to click into a fearsome attacking unit that saw crowds regularly surge in excess of 60,000. The missing piece of the jigsaw was not a player, it was

consistency – but City were now showing exactly that. Eric Brook and Ernie Toseland were once again supplying the ammunition, and Fred Tilson (when fit), Alex Herd and Doherty were all irrepressible.

Yet you could never be totally sure of what was to come next – a case in point being the 5-3 home loss to Grimsby Town on Christmas Day, which left Wild's team floundering in mid-table with only half the season to go. It was, however, to be the last defeat in what was to eventually prove an unbelievable run.

While the forward line was scoring at will, the defence – consisting of Percival, Bray, Barkas, Marshall and the legendary Frank Swift – were, at last, showing a meaner streak.

By mid-February, City still had much to do to close the gap on the leaders. Successive Tilson hat-tricks against Derby County and Wolves seemed to give the side the extra impetus needed to make a final push for the title. A crowd of more than 74,000 watched City beat fellow challengers Arsenal 2-0 in April and three more wins took the winning streak to seven in a row.

Wild's men had timed their assault to perfection and the title was won by three points, with Charlton Athletic the runners-up. The Championship trophy was on its way to Maine Road for the first time in the club's history. City fans floated on air with the knowledge that not only did they support the best team in Manchester, but also the whole country.

It had taken a while but Wild's men had also done it with style, the way City fans had demanded. Twelve months later, the unthinkable happened…

Above: City's long-serving manager Wilf Wild.

Right: Long-time captain Sam Cowan leads out the City team in the 1930s. He would later become the manager. .

Below: Ernest Mangnall's Manchester City squad of 1914/15. He is standing in the back row, fourth from the left.

Above right: City's forward line of 1913/14 (left to right): James Cumming, Harry Taylor, Fred Howard, Tommy Browell, Joe Cartwright

Right: : Bolton goalkeeper Dick Pym makes a save to deny City during the 1926 FA Cup final. Wanderers won the match at Wembley with a solitary goal.

"Manchester City's" Forward Line.

Cumming.   Taylor.   Howard.   Browell.   Cartwright.

Left: City's huge new ground in Moss Side, Manchester – Maine Road – is packed with thousands of fans as the Blues host Sheffield Wednesday in March 1934.

Above: HRH King George V is presented to the Manchester City team before the 1926 FA Cup Final. Captain Jimmy McMullan is the first to be greeted.

Above: City skipper Sam Cowan (left) and Everton captain Dixie Dean lead their team out for the 1933 FA Cup final at Wembley which the Blues lose 3-0.

Left: Legendary City goalkeeper Frank Swift gave City 16 years of loyal service, interrupted by World War 2 between 1933 and 1949.

Above: Newcastle United goalkeeper Sandy Mutch collects the ball as City's Horace Barnes threatens in the 1924 FA Cup semi-final at Birmingham's St Andrew's stadium. The Magpies triumph 2-0.

Left: Champions at last: Manager Wilf Wild sits proudly with the Football League Championship trophy and the rest of the 1936/37 squad.

SAM COWAN ROARED AT HIS TEAM-MATES TO SHOW THE SPIRIT NEEDED TO BECOME CHAMPIONS AND IT WORKED WONDERS AS THE BRILLIANT FRED TILSON SCORED TWO LATE SECOND-HALF GOALS (AFTER 74 AND 88 MINUTES) TO WIN THE GAME AND THE FA CUP FOR CITY 2-1.

Above: The City players are introduced to HRH King George V prior to the 1934 FA Cup final.

Left: City fans enjoying their day out in London ahead of the 1934 FA Cup final.

Below: Happy City fans gather around one of the fountains in London's Trafalgar square before going to Wembley to watch their heroes defeat Portsmouth 2-1 in the 1934 FA Cup final at Wembley.

BILLY MEREDITH

Billy Meredith may have played for City for the first time more than a century ago but his legend lives on to this day. Meredith – a somewhat controversial character – is ranked by many alongside the great Sir Stanley Matthews in stature and was a magnet for football fans and the media in his day. Bandy-legged and invariably chewing a toothpick – even when he played – Meredith was a fantastic player and the scourge of many an Edwardian defender. The immensely talented right-winger could pinpoint a cross for a forward or cut inside and lash the ball home himself if the mood took him.

He began life with Chirk in North Wales and then played for Northwich Victoria.

A former miner, Meredith was the driving force in City's early years and was integral to the club winning its first trophy. The 1904 FA Cup final was held at Crystal Palace in London and Meredith wasn't about to let this showpiece event pass him by. Twenty-three minutes in, he struck what would be the only goal of the game, to further enhance his reputation.

With 151 goals for the club, he is among the all-time top scorers for City, but his first spell would end in controversy and bitterness. He was involved in a bribe and illegal-payment scandal that rocked the club to its foundations. As a result, he eventually joined Manchester United, helping the Reds to the Division One title before City as he channeled his grievance into silverware for his new club.

He also organized the first meeting of what would eventually become the Professional Football Association (PFA) in 1907.

Yet Meredith, a lifelong teetotaler, felt he had unfinished business with City and, with time healing old wounds, he rejoined the Blues in 1921. Meredith was in his mid-forties by this point and past his best, but it was testament to his professionalism and fitness that he managed another 32 appearances for City and got to play at the club's new home, Maine Road. Not surprisingly, Meredith holds the record for being the oldest footballer to turn out for the Blues. He was aged just 120 days short of his 50th birthday in his last game for the club – a 2–0 defeat to Newcastle United in an FA Cup semi-final.

A true legend for not only City, but football in general.

MEREDITH, BILLY
1894–1905 and 1921–24
APPEARANCES
394
GOALS
151
POSITION
Winger
BORN
Chirk, North Wales

Left: Billy Meredith sits proudly with the FA Cup and the rest of his team-mates after their 1-0 FA Cup final win over Bolton Wanderers

Right: Billy Meredith (left), and team-mate Jack Warner, pictured in 1921, at the start of his second spell at Maine Road

TOMMY JOHNSON

Tommy Johnson might never have become a professional footballer if it wasn't for City defender Eli Fletcher. Johnson looked set for a different path when he began an apprenticeship at a shipyard near his Cumbrian home. Fletcher not only recommended Johnson to City, but actually threatened to leave the club if the youngster wasn't signed.

Johnson had to be patient for his opportunity to shine, finding his feet initially in the reserve team with more experienced forwards ahead of him in the pecking order.

It would be three more years before Johnson established himself fully in the Blues' starting line-up, forming an impressive partnership with Horace Barnes and going on to win two international caps for England while at City. He scored 20 or more goals for three successive seasons, but his tally of 38 league goals in 40 games in the 1928/29 season was easily his best and saw his stock rise even further. The hugely popular striker finally moved on to Everton in 1930 for £6,000, much to the supporters' chagrin – so much so that gates dropped by several thousand for a time afterwards, with many protesting against the sale. Ironically, Johnson played a large part in the 1933 FA Cup final win over City for Everton.

He forged a fearsome strike partnership with legendary striker Dixie Dean at Goodison Park, Everton's home ground, but he left a huge impression at City where he is behind only winger Eric Brook and striker Sergio Agüero in the list of all-time goal-scorers for the club – 166 goals from his 354 appearances. After his career ended, he became a publican and ran the Crown Inn in Gorton, never straying too far from Manchester.

JOHNSON, TOMMY
1919–30

APPEARANCES
354

GOALS
166

POSITION
Striker

BORN
Dalton-in-Furness

Left: The legendary City goal-scorer Tommy Johnson, whose record of 38 League goals in one campaign is still a Club record.

THE HUGELY POPULAR STRIKER FINALLY MOVED ON TO EVERTON IN 1930 FOR £6,000, MUCH TO THE SUPPORTERS' CHAGRIN – SO MUCH SO THAT GATES DROPPED BY SEVERAL THOUSAND FOR A TIME AFTERWARDS.

2. 1937–1964: RIVALRIES AND SUCCESSES

It's been often said that there really isn't another club like Manchester City.

Things happen, have happened and continue to happen that defy logic or reason, and the events that occurred during the 1937/38 season are undoubtedly the bedrock of such claims. To the present day, no defending champions of the English top division have been relegated the season after. Except for City.

The campaign began reasonably well with 4 wins and 3 defeats from the opening 8 matches, including a 6-1 win over Derby County. A tad inconsistent, but there were no alarm bells ringing. Eric Brook, Alex Herd and Peter Doherty were still scoring, albeit not quite with the regularity of the previous year, but the goals hadn't completely dried up.

Three wins from next 14 games, however, suggested something wasn't right and made City's hopes of retaining the title all but impossible. Yet there were flashes of brilliance: a 4-1 win over Leicester City and another drubbing of Derby County – 7-1 at the Baseball Ground – suggested all may not be lost and that, provided the Blues put in a superhuman effort, there was still the faintest of chances of glory.

However, it wasn't to be. Far from it, in fact. Six defeats and two draws in the next eight games again deflated the Maine Road fans, who hadn't even entertained the dreaded thought of relegation. Surely the champions of England couldn't be relegated... could they?

The FA Cup had provided welcome relief from the troubled campaign and City faced Aston Villa in the quarter-final at Villa Park. A crowd of more than 75,500 was treated to a cup thriller, but the Blues' last chance of silverware evaporated as Wild's team lost by the odd goal in five.

City entered April precariously placed above the drop zone. Successive wins over Charlton Athletic

and Chelsea at Maine Road were followed by defeats to Grimsby Town and Bolton Wanderers. The Blues were teetering to and fro on the relegation tightrope, blowing both hot and cold without warning.

If anything, City were infuriatingly inconsistent. Brook scored four times in a 7-1 win over West Bromwich Albion, and then the team lost to Bolton and drew with Charlton. Fans wondered how could they win with such ease one moment and flounder the next. This question has been asked many times over the years that have followed.

With two games remaining, City hammered Leeds United 6-2 at Maine Road and looked to have saved Wild's men from the ignominy of going down as champions. The final game, away to Huddersfield Town, gave City a further chance to save themselves and thousands of fans made their way across the Pennines to Leeds Road for a game that would see the losing side relegated. A draw would be enough to keep the Terriers up – could the Blues save themselves with one of those occasional blistering performances? The answer was no.

Huddersfield scored the only goal of the game and the unthinkable had happened. City were down, despite scoring 80 goals and conceding 77. Wilf Wild would, once again, have to inspire his men to recover from this devastating blow. He began by scouring the transfer market for players who could return his side to the top flight as quickly as possible.

It was a time of change as City began the 1938/39 season. It was Wilf Wild's seventh year in charge and the shock of being relegated as reigning champions was still only just sinking in.

The Blues began the campaign with more or less the same squad and began impressively with a 5-0 win over Swansea followed by a 3-0 victory over Chesterfield.

Above: Pre-season training
in the early 1950s included
jumping over park benches –
and there was no sponsored
training kit supplied – players
had to supply their own gear.

But the inability to go on a sustained run was again evident in the next four games – all defeats – with the 6-1 home loss to Millwall particularly poor.

Wild realized that a potent forward line was not enough to take the Blues back up to Division One and instead began to reshape his defence.

Full-backs Bert Sproston and Eric Westwood were signed from Spurs and Manchester United, respectively, and their steadying influence immediately inspired City to win five consecutive games in November. The goals were still flying in and wins of 9-3, 5-2 (both against Tranmere) and a 5-1 win over Bradford City were recorded in just four days at Christmas. The early season wobbles, however, meant that City were still off the pace of the leaders and, despite an unbeaten run of 10 games on the run-in, the Blues finished in a hugely disappointing fifth position, having scored 96 goals – two more than champions Blackburn Rovers. Only six players had managed to appear in more than 30 games in what was an unsettling time for the club, and for the rest of Britain.

On 1 September 1939, just three games into the new season, the Second World War began and the Football League programme was abandoned and results scratched from the records. A Western Regional League was set up, but many City players were called up for armed service duty as football became no more than a welcome distraction.

Games took on little more importance than friendlies and, even though gates would occasionally top 60,000, the majority of matches were witnessed by fewer than 10,000. Wilf Wild remained manager throughout the war, and when Britain and the allies finally defeated Hitler in 1945, the Football League reformed.

With the nation still celebrating the victory over Germany and the fortunate families welcoming the return of loved ones, Wilf Wild prepared City for the 1946/47 season. It would be his final campaign in charge as the Blues paved the way for the return of a favourite son. With the war over, the British public slowly tried to return to some kind of normality, and football had its part to play. City began where they'd left off, in Division Two – effectively for the past eight years.

Jimmy Constantine, who had hit 25 goals in 34 games for the Blues during the Second World War, was now the star striker, and the excellent Joe Fagan, who had signed just before the Football League had been suspended in 1939, would provide solidity across the back line with able support from goalkeeper Frank Swift and full-backs Sam Barkas and Bert Sproston.

Above: Dave Ewing and the diving Newcastle's Vic Keeble clash during the 1955 FA Cup final.

The great Peter Doherty had left for Derby County after several disagreements with City's hierarchy during wartime, but the Blues began the season at a pace, with successive wins over Leicester City and Bury.

The Maine Road crowds were averaging around 40,000 and City finished September still unbeaten, with four wins and three draws. It was vital that the club return to the top division as soon as possible and, following a couple of losses in October, the board of directors, with the 52-year-old Wilf Wild's blessing, invited a former legend to manage the club.

Sam Cowan had played more than 400 times for the Blues from 1924–35 and was still fondly remembered by all at Maine Road. He had settled on the south coast and set up a thriving physiotherapy practice when the call came from City.

Cowan accepted the role and so ended Wild's amazing 14-year reign as Blues boss. Cowan's impact was immediate, and City set off on a record-breaking run of 22 games without defeat, including 14 clean sheets – seemingly gone were the days of throwing caution to the wind... for the time being, anyway.

With 17 wins and five draws, Cowan had guided City to the top of the table, often playing in front of 60,000-plus crowds. He was every bit as much

a hero as a manager as he had been as a player and, despite the hiccup of three losses from the final seven games, City were crowned champions of Division Two, winning their final game 5-1 at home to Newport, with all five goals scored by George Smith, and finishing four points ahead of runners-up Burnley.

During his brief reign, Cowan had continued the 260-mile commute to his home in Hove – a journey that could take between six and eight hours by road or rail. Not unreasonably, the directors at Maine Road weren't happy with the arrangement, which was tiring for their manager and also wasted many hours in travel.

Perhaps feeling they held all the aces, the board stood firm and, when no agreement could be reached – and in spite of his achievements – Cowan left the Blues shortly after the final game of the season. The City fans were understandably dismayed, but Cowan was equally stubborn, and the impasse left the club, once again, looking for a manager. How far Cowan might have taken the club will never be known.

The ever dependable Wilf Wild filled the void once more while City searched for a new man, and the first game of the season saw the Blues defeat Wolves 4-3 at Maine Road in an exhilarating match

IT WAS A TRANSITIONAL PERIOD FOR THE CLUB, WITH MANY ESTABLISHED STARS COMING TO THE END OF THEIR CAREERS. WITH THE BLUES HAVING WON DIVISION 2 AT A CANTER IN THE PREVIOUS CAMPAIGN, MUCH WAS EXPECTED OF THE SIDE.

Right: Forward Bobby Johnstone scored in both the 1955 (the defeat against Newcastle United) and 1956 (victory over Birmingham City) FA Cup finals for City.

watched by 67,800. Football was enjoying amazing attendances as the country began to enjoy life again following the war, and the September Manchester derby attracted a massive 78,000 to Maine Road to witness a 0-0 draw.

Wild would remain in the hot-seat until November when former Everton wing-half John "Jock" Thomson agreed to take over. The 41-year-old Scot had helped Everton beat City in the 1933 FA Cup final and took over a team in mid-table with 16 points from a possible 34 giving him a base to build upon.

It was a transitional period for the club, with many established stars coming to the end of their careers. With the Blues having won Division Two at a canter in the previous campaign, much was expected of the side.

Influential skipper Sam Barkas had retired as a player after almost 200 appearances for City and became Workington Town's new boss when there had perhaps been a strong case for him taking over from Cowan. Future Liverpool legend Joe Fagan was becoming the defensive lynchpin of the side, while Thomson opted for the productive strike force of Andy Black and George Smith, ably supported by the exciting left-wing talents of Roy Clarke.

But inconsistency was, once again, the Blues' main issue and it would be March before City would string together successive wins, finishing the season with no wins in the final six matches.

On the plus side, finishing in 10th place was no disgrace and a fair achievement for a promoted club, but there had been little to suggest the side was progressing in the right direction.

The carefree attitude of the Blues seemed a distant memory going into the 1948/49 season. Gone were the high-scoring games and glut of goals of the recent past, replaced by a more defensive-minded approach to games. By the 10th match of the campaign, City were averaging just

over a goal a game and had racked up four clean sheets. Maine Road crowds were consistently in excess of 40,000 but the entertainment being served was not to the taste of everyone at the club, with "the Great Unpredictables" edging toward stability. The home derby again ended 0-0, watched by 64,502, but the spark of excitement and never being quite sure of what was going to happen was absent for City fans. The consistency that had been missing from the previous season was at least evident in defence, where City were becoming a mean outfit, but goals were increasingly hard to come by. Following a 3-2 win on New Year's Day against Stoke City, the Blues scored just 11 times in 16 games, twice winning three successive games 1-0 during that period.

Only Smith and Black reached double figures, and City's final goals-scored total of just 47 from 42 games and 16 without a goal told its own story. Thomson's side had finished in seventh place but, again, something wasn't quite right. The tactics weren't overly popular – City fans didn't do dull or predictable, but things would get worse before they got better, and the next 12 months would prove to be a miserable affair for the Blues' fans.

Manchester City were limping into the new decade under the reins of Jock Thomson and the 1949/50 season began as it would end – poorly. There were no real stars in the side anymore and, although gates at Maine Road regularly topped 50,000, the Blues were again on their way down.

Frank Swift was coming to the end of an illustrious career with the club and Thomson had made a brave decision to bring a young German goalkeeper to Moss Side, barely four years after the Second World War.

Bert Trautmann had been a prisoner-of-war during the conflict but had decided to stay in England following his release. The former paratrooper worked on a farm for a while before

marrying a local girl. Word had spread of his talent while playing for St Helens Town, but it was the Blues who were the boldest and actually took a massive gamble and signed him.

The decision caused an outcry and dismay, with the wounds of the war still very raw and feeling of hostility to Germany still fresh. Trautmann made his debut in a poor City team and was helpless to stop Bolton win 3-0. He kept a clean sheet on his home debut – a 4-0 victory over Birmingham City – but the next game saw Derby put seven past him!

The sequence of results pretty much summed up the Blues that season and a run of four wins from the final 23 games – during which Thompson was dismissed – ensured City's return to Division Two. It had been a controversial, colourless campaign and the club were, once more, looking for a man who could bring stability back to Maine Road.

Sam Cowan's brief but successful reign as team boss convinced the board to look for someone who understood the club and its supporters. The answer lay roughly 50 miles away, where former skipper Les McDowall was managing Wrexham. He fitted the bill perfectly.

In June 1950, McDowall agreed to become City's new manager. It was the start of a long and successful era for the India-born boss, whose first task was to take the Blues back to Division One.

McDowall's first match in charge was a precursor of the exciting times ahead. The Blues beat Preston North End 4-2 at Deepdale with Smith (2), Westcott and Clarke on the scoresheet. It was followed by a midweek victory over Cardiff and more than 40,000 Maine Road fans saw City thrash Bury 5-1 just three days later. McDowall's men remained unbeaten in their first 10 games, scoring freely while looking solid at the back, thanks largely to new signing Roy Paul.

The strapping half-back was a real *Roy of the Rovers*-type defender – brave, popular, hugely talented and carved out of Welsh granite. Indeed,

as a former coalminer, he had known life down the pits and appreciated football giving him a way out. McDowall paid Swansea Town £25,000 for his services – a tidy sum for the time – but Paul was worth every penny.

City's good form continued and, by the middle of November, the club were top of the league and looking a strong bet for an instant return to Division One. But City wouldn't be City if they didn't make things difficult for themselves and, following a 4-1 drubbing at Blackburn, McDowall's men won just four times in the next 17 games.

Worse still, the club's legendary secretary and former manager, Wilf Wild, passed away aged 57. Few men had served Manchester City with greater distinction and his loss was mourned by all connected with the club.

Above left: Talented and prolific striker Don Revie poses for a pre-season photo.

Above: The legendary Frank Swift – a magnificent goalkeeper and a gentle giant off the pitch – who tragically died, working as a journalist, in the 1958 Munich air disaster.

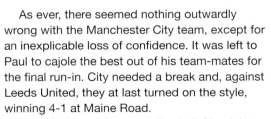

had topped the table earlier in the campaign, or the stuttering bunch of individuals that threatened to derail the promotion express.

Fortunately, it was the former and City were outstanding, winning 6-0. The win virtually assured the runners-up spot, but three successive draws to complete the season had Blues fans biting their nails all the way to the end, when promotion was finally guaranteed.

Would City fans want it any other way?

The Blues had returned to Division One but, after an unconvincing start to the 1951/52 campaign, McDowall scoured the country for reinforcements and signed Ken Branagan, exciting forward Ivor Broadis and the highly rated Don Revie. Both Branagan and Revie cost City around £25,000 – record fees for the club and not far short of the British record for transfer fees paid.

The deals were possible thanks to the huge Maine Road crowds City regularly played in front of and a solid board who believed McDowall could make City a force to be reckoned with again. All three new signings played together for the first time in mid-October during a 0-0 draw at Burnley. The Blues then won their next three games to begin their move to a more comfortable mid-table position.

By early January, the Blues were in the top 10 and moving along nicely but, for no obvious reason, they won only one of their final 17 league and cup matches to finish a disappointing 15th. Still, at least a place among the nation's elite had been preserved, but the question all City fans must have been wondering was: for how long?

The 1952/53 campaign proved a topsy-turvy one for the Blues. McDowall was still some way short of finding his best line-up but was prepared to experiment with different formations and tactics from time to time. In view of how City began the season, it was amazing that the McDowall was still in charge at all by the end of October. His team were, at times, awful and, even though three games

As ever, there seemed nothing outwardly wrong with the Manchester City team, except for an inexplicable loss of confidence. It was left to Paul to cajole the best out of his team-mates for the final run-in. City needed a break and, against Leeds United, they at last turned on the style, winning 4-1 at Maine Road.

The win seemed to spark the belief back into the Blues and, following a 0-0 draw at home to Notts County, they won three successive games to vault them back into the promotion frame. Defeat at Southampton added even more pressure on the home fixture with Barnsley, who had already held City 1-1 at Oakwell earlier in the season.

A crowd of 42,741 turned up wondering which Manchester City was going to run out on to the Maine Road pitch – the slick attacking outfit that

in they beat United 2-1, it would be the only league win in the first 16 matches. City were rooted to the bottom of the table and seemingly destined for relegation yet again.

Maine Road was still packing the fans in but a 5-2 home loss to Sunderland, followed by a 7-3 defeat to Wolves, must have tested their patience to the limit. Yet, from somewhere, the Blues found the stomach for the battle ahead.

A 5-1 win over Charlton restored a modicum of confidence but City still found travelling painful and were beaten in their next game at Highbury. If the club had, at last, found some belief, it was only when they played at Maine Road and they set off on an incredible run of 10 successive home wins, picking up the occasional point or two away, as well as the odd thrashing too.

By mid-April, the club was just above the relegation zone and was faced with a visit from the mighty Arsenal. The Gunners were too powerful on the day and ended City's magnificent run with a 4-2 victory. Defeats at Derby and to Preston at home had left the McDowall's men staring bleakly at Division Two football again but, with two games to go, destiny was still in the Blues' own hands.

The visit of Blackpool represented the best chance of gaining the desperately needed points, but the Seasiders had already administered a 4-1 thrashing at Bloomfield Road earlier in the season and were more than capable of repeating the performance with their talented side.

Almost 40,000 had turned up to cheer their heroes and, on this occasion, home advantage gave the Blues the edge. It was typical of City to save their best performance for their penultimate game of the season and, by the final whistle, City had scored five without reply.

The Blues were safe and the 3-1 defeat at Chelsea on the final day didn't matter. They'd escaped the drop by the skin of their teeth, but escaped they had.

The question was, had the lessons of the previous campaign been learned? City began the 1953/54 campaign with a run of results that again suggested a long, painful nine months ahead.

Manager McDowall had been toying with giving the talented, but hardly prolific striker Revie a new role within the side. The poor start to the campaign convinced him to give what would become known as "The Revie Plan" a go.

Above: "The Popular Side" – which would later become the Kippax – was packed to capacity and without a roof in its early years – not ideal in the "Rainy City"!

Above: Roy Clarke gave 11 seasons of loyal service, making 349 appearances for City between 1947 and 1958.

Right: (left to right) Youngsters Glyn Pardoe, Alf Wood and G. Howard smile for the camera in a 1963/64 pre-season photoshoot. Howard would never make a first-team appearance for the Blues, Pardoe, 378 and Wood 31.

It meant that Revie would play in a position behind the forward line but ahead of the midfielders, thus making him somewhat elusive to the defenders of the day to mark.

It would be some time before the City players themselves became used to the system, but they would stick with the formation inspired by the all-conquering Hungarian side of the early 1950s.

By Christmas, the Blues were, once again, in trouble, having won just five of their 24 Division One games. McDowall tinkered with his personnel and tactics in a bid to turn the tide with little effect, but there was enough talent in the team to grind out a series of draws and narrow wins to stave off the threat of relegation.

With Revie in a more withdrawn role, Johnny Hart needed a new strike partner and McDowall signed Irish forward Billy McAdams in January 1954 to bolster the attack. McAdams scored a hat-trick on only his second appearance for the Blues as City progressed to the next round of the FA Cup against Bradford City.

He would end the season with 11 goals in 19 appearances, just one behind joint top scorers Revie and Hart as City finished in 17th position. It wasn't the best of times at Maine Road but brighter days were just around the corner.

The 1954/55 campaign was steady and saw the Blues reach the FA Cup final for the first time in 21 years, but fate handed the trophy to Newcastle United. Jackie Milburn scored after just 45 seconds – the quickest goal Wembley had ever seen – and things soon got worse for the Blues. With no subs allowed, full-back Jimmy Meadows was taken off with a career-ending leg injury after just 17 minutes and City were down to 10 men, but Bobby Johnstone still managed to level the scores on the stroke of half-time. The Magpies added two more goals shortly after the break to ensure the trophy went to the north east for the third time in five years. Just as Sam Cowan had done in 1933,

captain Roy Paul promised to return to Wembley the following May and lift the cup.

City dusted themselves down from the disappointment of losing the final against Newcastle but began the 1955/56 season like a team with a severe hangover. Two 2-2 draws and a 7-2 hammering at Wolves must have left boss McDowall wondering where his side were heading. It was only a temporary blip, as Paul set about waking his team-mates up to the job in hand with great effect with a 1-0 win over United in front of nearly 60,000 fans at Maine Road.

By Christmas, the Blues were sat in mid-table looking at another unremarkable season. At least Paul had the FA Cup prophecy to focus on and, hopefully, fulfil. City had drawn Blackpool at home and were level at 1-1 when the game was abandoned due to severe weather. The match was replayed four days later, with Bobby Johnstone and Jackie Dyson scoring the goals in a 2-1 win. Southend away was a tightly fought tie, with Joe Hayes scoring the only goal of the game at Roots Hall. So far, so good.

The Blues' league form also picked up and McDowall's men were climbing the table accordingly. A home fifth-round pairing with Second Division Liverpool seemed a comfortable draw and 70,640 fans packed Maine Road to cheer their heroes into the last 16, but the Reds clung on for a 0-0 draw and City instead progressed with victory at Anfield following goals from Hayes and Dyson that clinched a 2-1 win – and a home draw with Everton for the sixth round.

Cup fever was gripping the City fans and more than 76,000 watched a 2-1 home win over the Toffees, with goals from Hayes and Johnstone.

Two games from glory, Paul was not about to let his dream slip away and he was inspirational in the semi-final as City beat Spurs 1-0 to return to Wembley for the second successive year. Their opponents would be Birmingham City, who had

WITH NO REPLACEMENT ALLOWED, TRAUTMANN STAYED IN GOAL TO SEE OUT THE REMAINING MINUTES, ALTHOUGH IT TRANSPIRED HE HAD BROKEN HIS NECK. CITY HELD OUT, HOWEVER, TO WIN 3-1.

already beaten and drawn with City earlier in the campaign.

The Blues wound-up their league season finishing an impressive fourth – the best for 20 years – now for the cup final. A late injury to Billy Spurdle meant a chance for Don Revie to play. McDowall had employed the Revie Plan in the final against Newcastle and had been roundly criticized for doing so – but he was determined to prove the doubters wrong.

Hayes gave City a dream start, with a goal after two minutes, but Kinsey equalized for Birmingham after quarter of an hour. Revie was causing all kinds of problems for the Midlands club and he again played a part in City's second goal, scored by Dyson midway through the second half. Two minutes later and City were 3-1 up through Bobby Johnstone and the victory was effectively sealed. But there was more drama to come. At 75 minutes, Bert Trautmann made a typically brave save at the feet of Brum striker Peter Murphy, who caught the big German's neck with his knee in the ensuing collision. Trautmann was treated for several minutes before soldiering on in great agony.

With no replacement allowed, Trautmann stayed in to see out the remaining minutes, although it transpired he had actually broken his neck. City held out, however, to win 3-1. Paul collected the FA Cup, just as he'd promised he would, and the Blues returned to Manchester as heroes – but none more so than Trautmann, whose bravery would never be forgotten by the City fans.

The FA Cup success would be City's last high for several seasons.

City finished the 1956/67 campaign just above relegation in 18th place and Bobby Johnstone top scoring with 16 strikes from 31 league games. Bert Trautmann had made an amazing recovery from his broken neck and played every game of the second half of the season.

The 1957/58 campaign proved more fruitful but,

with Don Revie now departed, McDowall instead attempted the "Marsden Plan" – based around former Chesterfield half-back Keith Marsden – but it resulted in disastrous losses of 6-1 at Preston and 9-2 at West Brom in successive games. Jack Savage, the City keeper standing in for Trautmann, had come in for some severe punishment from supporters and left the club shortly after.

It was an incredible season in many ways, with a ridiculous amount of goals at both ends of the pitch. By the end, City had scored 104 and conceded 100 goals – the only time this feat has ever happened before or since.

Finishing fifth in the campaign, with Joe Hayes top scoring with 25 goals, it was to be the last time McDowall would steer his troops into the top 10, as several seasons of average football followed with finishes of 20th, 15th, 13th, 12th and, in 1962/63, 21st, resulting in relegation.

McDowall had been in charge for 13 years and had never really managed to make City a major force in that time, the 1956 FA Cup triumph being his only real legacy. The side was in a transitional period between a crop of emerging youngsters and a group of seasoned pros coming to the end of their careers.

Given the need for a freshening up of the old guard, George Poyser – McDowall's assistant for the previous six years – was installed as the new City boss, but things were about to get even bleaker.

Poyser was unable to resurrect the Blues' fortunes but, as a respected scout and champion of youth football, he nurtured the precocious talents of the next generation of City stars, with Alan Oakes, Neil Young, Dave Connor, Glyn Pardoe and Mike Doyle all featuring in Poyser's two seasons in charge, neither of which saw City trouble the promotion challengers.

In fact, the 11th-place finish in the 1964/65 season was City's lowest ever finishing position.

Things had to change, as the Club was aimlessly drifting toward mediocrity.

Above: Les McDowall's former assistant George Poyser got his chance to manage between 1963 to 1965 but it was a difficult time for the Club and there was little resource available. Poyser still managed to unearth some homegrown gems who became integral to Joe Mercer's side a few years later.

THE 1954/55 CAMPAIGN WAS STEADY AND SAW THE BLUES REACH THE FA CUP FINAL FOR THE FIRST TIME IN 21 YEARS, BUT FATE HANDED THE TROPHY TO NEWCASTLE UNITED.

Above: Newcastle keeper Ronnie Simpson claws the ball away as Don Revie threatens in the 1955 FA Cup Final at Wembley.

Right: Jimmy Meadows clears the danger as Newcastle look to build on their first minute goal in the 1955 FA Cup final. Meadows would soon have to leave the pitch with injury and with no subs allowed, City were reduced to 10 men for the remainder of the game, eventually losing 3-1

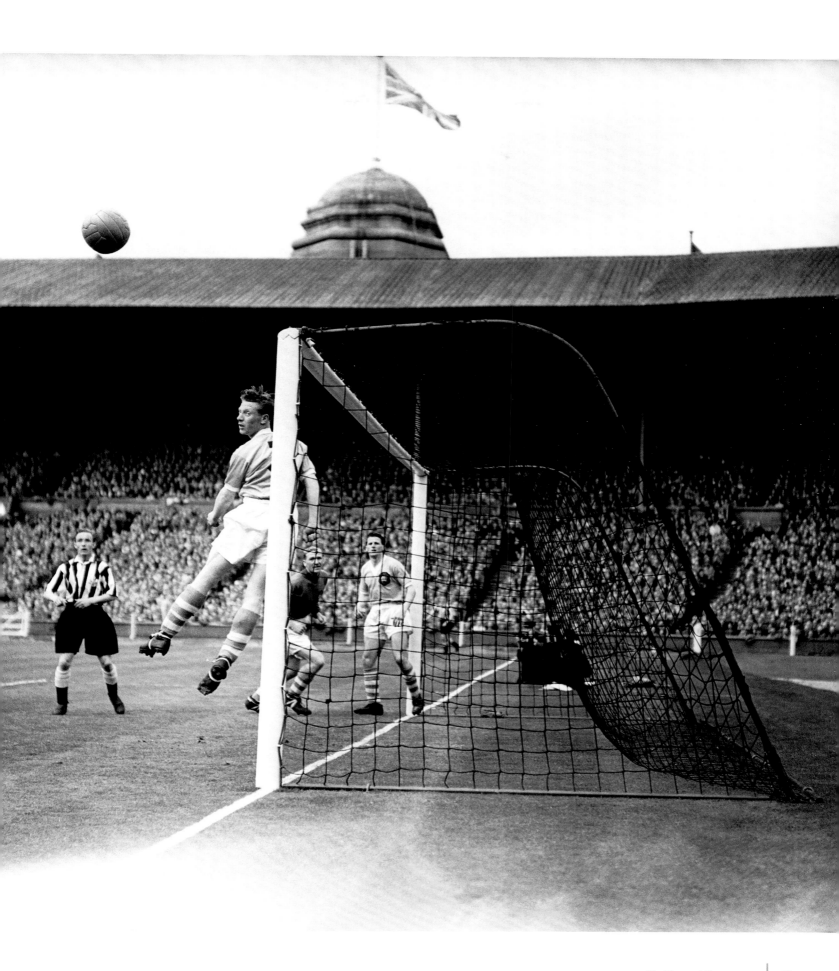

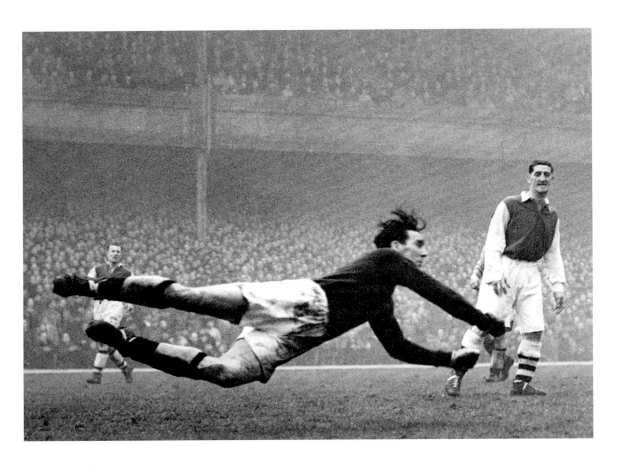

Above: Frank Swift at full stretch makes sure there is no danger from this Arsenal attack at Highbury in 1948.

Left: : Don Revie in action during the 1955 FA Cup semi-final with Sunderland at Villa Park. Roy Clarke's goal won it for City 1-0.

Right: Manager Les McDowall (left) and the talented City team who went on to win the 1956 FA Cup final against Birmingham City.

Below: Bert Trautmann watches on as City take on Blackpool at Bloomfield Road. City lose the 1953/54 clash 2-0

Left: Hero – Bert Trautmann, still in agony after breaking his neck, leaves the pitch after the final whistle in the 1956 FA Cup final..

Below: The moment Birmingham City's Peter Murphy's knee collides with Bert Trautmann's neck, severely injuring the brave German keeper who insisted that he play on for the remainder of the game.

Above: Bobby Johnstone scores for the second FA Cup final in a row, this time to put City 2-1 up against Birmingham City.

Centre: City captain Roy Paul leads out the team beofre the 1956 FA Cup final. As both teams wore blue shirts, City changed to burgundy and yellow striped shirts and Birminingham to white shirts.

Right: Bobby Johnstone watches as the ball hits the back of the net to give the Blues the lead.

Top left: Bert Trautmann and a stellar cast of guests at his testimonial (including Stanley Matthews) in April 1964. Almost 48,000 fans turn out to pay homage to the German legend.

Middle left: Don Revie drinks champagne from the FA Cup after City's 3-1 win over Birmingham City at Wembley in 1956.

Above: The talented Roy Clarke in 1955/56. Signed from Cardiff, the Welsh winger made 370 appearances and scored 70 goals from 1947 to 1958.

Left: Frank Swift is carried off shoulder-high by his team-mates after his final game before retirement, a goalless draw with Everton in September 1949.

POYSER WAS UNABLE TO RESURRECT THE
BLUES' FORTUNES BUT, AS A RESPECTED
SCOUT AND CHAMPION OF YOUTH FOOTBALL,
HE NURTURED THE PRECOCIOUS TALENTS OF
THE NEXT GENERATION OF CITY STARS.

Above: George Poyser and
his young Manchester City
side of 1963/64. Relegated
from Division 1 the previous
season, City bounced back
as champions in 1956/66.

ROY PAUL

It's no exaggeration to say Roy Paul was Manchester City's very own Captain Fantastic. An inspirational figure to colleagues and fans alike, he was a true leader and, without doubt, one of the best players to ever wear a Manchester City shirt.

After leaving school he, like many of his friends and family in the Welsh valleys, became a miner and looked set for a life down the pits. His talent at football, however, soon offered him a different pathway, and Swansea offered him a contract when he was aged just 19. He duly accepted the opportunity. The outbreak of war meant his debut was put on hold for six years, during which time he served in the Marines as a P.E. instructor in Devon and India.

When he returned to the pitch, Paul proved he was a tough as the coalface he used to mine and a fearful figure for any opposition forward to face. He quickly became Swansea's most prized asset and when the second-tier Swans faced a powerful Arsenal side in a 1950 FA Cup tie, the Gunners immediately placed a bid for Paul, so impressive was the Welsh defender. The bid was turned down, though Paul later angered the Swansea board when he accepted the offer of a trial with Colombian side Millonarios, with a lucrative contract on offer if all went to plan. Paul remained in Colombia for just 10 days before heading home to South Wales where he was promptly transfer-listed.

The recently relegated City wasted no time securing his signature for £19,500 and Paul suddenly had the platform his ability deserved. The Welshman was swiftly made captain as promotion was secured at the first attempt.

A genuine *Roy of the Rovers*-type player, Paul went on to be one of the greatest captains the club has ever had, and led the Blues to the 1955 FA Cup final, where they lost to Newcastle United. As Sam Cowan had done before him, he vowed to return to win the Cup the next year. Paul didn't disappoint, and led the Blues to the 1956 FA Cup final, where this time City were victorious over Birmingham City.

In their first three FA Cup triumphs, two City captains had been Welshmen – the first was Billy Meredith – and the triumph was just reward for a career that perhaps deserved more. Paul left for Southern League Worcester City in June 1957, believing the pace he'd lost made it increasingly hard to defend the way he had and, after clocking up nearly 300 matches for City, the club reluctantly agreed with his decision.

At Worcester, Paul had one more moment of FA Cup glory in 1959, leading his team to a shock defeat of Liverpool. He died in the spring of 2002.

PAUL, ROY
1950–1957

APPEARANCES
293

GOALS
8

POSITION
Half-back

BORN
Ton Pentre, Wales

Right: Proud as Punch! Roy Paul, sitting on Don Revie's shoulders, made good on his promise to take City back to Wembley after losing the 1955 FA Cup final and win it in 1956.

A GENUINE *ROY OF THE ROVERS-*TYPE PLAYER, PAUL WENT ON TO BE ONE OF THE GREATEST CAPTAINS THE CLUB HAS EVER HAD.

ERIC BROOK

Eric Brook scored 177 goals in 453 appearances for City between 1928 and 1940, and led the scoring charts after overtaking Tom Johnson's total of 166 with a goal away to Bradford City in September 1938 until Sergio Agüero broke his record in 2017.

There is no doubt that Brook was a special player and a fantastic signing for City. A left-winger by trade, Brook rarely stayed on the flanks and considered the position as somewhere to find his bearings, but any right-back hoping to man-mark Brook from start to finish would likely leave a big hole on one side of the defence, as the City "winger" had a licence to roam – and roam he did.

Brook cut a powerful figure and was physically imposing and strong. He possessed one of the most powerful shots of his era and would regularly thump home penalties with venom. Though he won just 18 England caps, many believe he was one of the best players of the late 1920s and 1930s and that perhaps he didn't get the recognition he deserved.

Born in Mexborough, Yorkshire, in 1907, Brook signed for Barnsley as a teenager and remained with the Tykes for three years before City came in with an offer of £6,000 for Brook and his team-mate, Fred Tilson, in March 1928 – an inspired move by manager Peter Hodge, with Tilson's 132 career goals for the Blues meaning the pair would net an incredible 309 goals between them in a combined appearance total of 726 matches – not bad value for money!

Brook and Tilson joined Tom Johnson, Billy Austin and Frank Roberts to form one of the most lethal forward lines in English football and, although he played only 12 times, Brook played his part as the Blues won promotion from Division Two.

Brook quickly became integral in City's side, scoring 14 goals in 42 league appearances during his first full campaign at Maine Road and achieving double figures in goals during his first five seasons, rarely missing a game. But for Arsenal's Cliff Bastin, he would likely have doubled his appearances for England, but the pair were considered too similar in their style and only played in the same side a few times.

City lifted the FA Cup in 1934, with Brook assisting the winning goal for Tilson, and were crowned champions of England in 1937. Brook rarely missed a game in either campaign and scored twice in the 4-1 win over Sheffield Wednesday at Maine Road to clinch the title, watched by a crowd of more than 55,000. Maybe only as City could back then, the Blues outscored every other side in the top flight, but were relegated as defending champions – the only time this has ever happened in English football – and the 1938/39 campaign in Division Two would be Brook's last full season for the Blues.

He played three games of the 1939/40 season before the Second World War meant the league was suspended and the games and the one goal he scored scratched from the record books. Though he made a handful of wartime appearances in 1939, a car crash left him with a fractured skull and, unable to head the ball again, he was forced to retire at the relatively young age of 32.

BROOK, ERIC
1928–40

APPEARANCES
453

GOALS
177

POSITION
Winger

BORN
Mexborough

CARRERAS CIGARETTES

E. BROOK
MANCHESTER C. (1ST DIV.)

Left: Eric Brook, posing for a photo in 1929/30, was City's record goal-scorer for 79 years until Sergio Agüero overtook his tally of 177 goals.

Right: Cigarette cards were highly collectable. On the back of the card, such as this Eric Brook one from 1934, would be a brief biography.

BERT TRAUTMANN

Bert Trautmann overcame virtually every hurdle you could possibly imagine in his rise to becoming one of the most popular players ever to play for the Blues, going on to become a legendary figure and, if not the best goalkeeper the club has had, almost certainly the bravest. Bert was a German paratrooper during the Second World War and was captured in Normandy and then made a prisoner-of-war.

From the POW camp in Ashton-in-Makerfield, he tried his hand at goalkeeping. His training as a paratrooper had served him well, as he would later claim that it helped him to cushion the ball as he fell. Whatever the reasons, it worked.

He was released after the war and decided to stay in England, eventually finding work on a farm. He played for St Helens FC and, shortly after, married the club secretary's daughter. Word had spread of the German goalkeeper with huge promise and City soon signed him up, putting him straight into the first team. With the war still fresh in everyone's minds, it is perhaps understandable that City fans were, at first, resentful of the German's presence in the team, especially as he was the replacement for the great Frank Swift, who had recently retired.

While City fans gradually warmed to the big German, fans of other clubs took longer to accept him, though there were several occasions when the jeers turned to respectful applause as Trautmann turned in some amazing displays.

Once they saw past their own prejudices, people were quick to see him as a man with the heart of a lion. Incredibly, while helping City to a 1956 FA Cup final victory over Birmingham, Bert dived bravely at Birmingham striker Peter Murphy's legs and hurt himself badly as he collided with his knee. The City goalkeeper was in tremendous pain but, with

no substitutes allowed, the only option other than leaving the field of play was to continue – and it was the latter that he chose. He had, in fact, broken his neck but, despite the obvious agony he was in, wanted to make sure his team-mates got over the line and won the FA Cup.

His team-mates did all they could to protect him in the final 15 minutes or so and City won the game 3-1. It was that kind of heroism that guaranteed Trautmann almost mythical status among the City fans, and at Bert's testimonial, a huge crowd of more than 47,000 turned up to pay their respects. The word "legendary" could have been invented for Bert – a giant of a man in every respect.

TRAUTMANN, BERT
1949–64
APPEARANCES
545
GOALS
0
POSITION
Goalkeeper
BORN
Bremen, Germany

Left: Bert Trautmann, under pressure from Arsenal centre-forward Tommy Lawton, punches clear at Highbury in 1953.

Right: Bert Trautmann – one of City's all-time greats – calmly waits for the start of the Blues' Division 1 match against Tottenham Hotspur at White Hart Lane in 1956.

3. 1964–1982: LEE, BELL AND SUMMERBEE

Joe Mercer had enjoyed an illustrious playing career with Everton and Arsenal before a broken leg forced his retirement and robbed him of more playing years – but he was far from finished with football. His first move into management was with Sheffield United and he impressed sufficiently to be made Aston Villa boss. He took them to promotion from Division Two, won the League Cup and led them to two FA Cup semi-finals. The pressures and stress of management, however, took their toll on Joe and he suffered a mild stroke. He made a full recovery but, despite the doctors giving him a clean bill of health, the Villa board sacked him. Understandably disappointed, he decided to retire, and many thought they had seen the last of "Genial Joe". But Mercer's love of the game pulled him back and, in 1965, when Manchester City offered him the opportunity of waking a sleeping giant, he grabbed the chance with both hands. It was to prove a match made in heaven.

His first move was to bring promising young coach Malcolm Allison to City as his assistant and, though the pair were like chalk and cheese, they would prove the perfect managerial team and as good as any in the history of English football.

Allison was brash, flamboyant and an innovative coach, and he complemented Mercer's father-figure approach perfectly. City had the makings of a decent team with homegrown talent such as Neil Young, Dave Connor, Glyn Pardoe, Mike Doyle and Alan Oakes all emerging. Winger Mike Summerbee arrived from Swindon Town, while exciting prospect Colin Bell also joined during the season from Bury.

From a listless, drifting giant to a slick young side with an enviable management team, City's future looked rosy again and the football and feel-good factor was back at Maine Road. Optimism – a rarely used word at the time – was back in the air for the first time since Sam Cowan's return to the club after the war.

Since then, bar a couple of notable highs, City had been on a steady decline, but Mercer and Allison re-energized the club, players and supporters, and the new-look City went on to be win the Division Two championship for a record sixth time after a 3-2 win at Charlton Athletic confirmed the title.

With City crowned Division Two champions in the first season under Joe Mercer, the customary expectation levels that supporters of Manchester City have were raised once again and, after a fairly miserable decade, who could blame them?

Allison was a big hit with the players and Mercer provided the more respected, public face of the management team. It was Allison who pushed for the signing of a player who, at 32, seemed to lack top-level experience in football and was – quite frankly – a gamble at what is an advanced age for a footballer.

But Allison convinced Mercer that Tony Book was the man to lead City back to the glory days and, in July 1966, the Plymouth Argyle defender joined the Blues (later claiming that Allison had told him to say he was two years younger to ensure the deal got over the line!). With the promising local youngsters all blossoming, plus Bell and Summerbee already looking like bargain buys, the Blues began the 1966/67 season with high expectations of their own.

More than 50,000 packed Maine Road for the opening home game of the season and they left smiling after goals from Bell and Jimmy Murray gave them a 2-1 win over Liverpool. Another home win over Sunderland three days later saw City loftily placed in the first published league table.

Six defeats in the next eight soon dampened the early enthusiasm and some wondered if the

Above: Neil Young hammers home the winning goal to secure the 1-0 win over Leicester City in the 1969 FA Cup final at Wembley..

Right: : Francis Lee scampers down the flank at Maine Road.

club was even heading straight back down again. Were it not for the handful of points in the autumn, they may well have been. A miserable Christmas and New Year period with the Blues failing to score in four league games hardly helped matters, but they weren't conceding too many either.

The feeling was that they were probably just a couple of players short of being a very good side. Mercer already had a few ideas on who he'd like to bring in and Allison targeted a winger and a striker who he felt were the missing pieces of the jigsaw. City only conceded one goal on four occasions during their last 24 games, but they weren't scoring too many at the other end either. An appearance in the FA Cup quarter-final, where they lost 1-0 to Leeds United, and a final placing of 15th in the league represented a decent enough return to the top flight, but Mercer and Allison wanted more from their young side.

Winger Tony Coleman was added in March 1967, providing additional firepower down the flanks, but the team still wasn't complete.

The 1967/68 began with a 0-0 draw at home to Liverpool and was followed by successive defeats at Southampton and Stoke, but five wins on the bounce was encouraging. Successive defeats to United, Arsenal and Sunderland had the management team scratching their heads again, but the final piece of the jigsaw was about to be added as the Blues captured highly rated Bolton forward Francis Lee for £60,000 – the team was complete.

Lee's first 11 league appearances for City resulted in eight wins and 3 draws. He also scored 8 times as his new club raced toward the top of the table. With Tony Book's leadership, plus Mike

Doyle, Glyn Pardoe, George Heslop and Alan Oakes outstanding in defence, the Blues were able to express themselves in the last two-thirds of the pitch, and they certainly had the players to do exactly that.

Mike Summerbee, Colin Bell, Neil Young, Tony Coleman and new boy Lee were a daunting prospect for any defence to face and, as City left the pitch at Reading having won an FA Cup replay 7-0 in January 1968, the PA announcer told the home fans they had "just seen the best team in England."

He was spot-on.

The forwards and midfielders were all chipping in with goals and the defence rarely let in more than one goal. Defeat at Leeds in March was followed with a triumphant 3-1 win at Manchester United and it was perhaps this victory that would prove as crucial as any on the run-in.

The next five games brought delight at home with wins over Chelsea and West Ham but despair away with two defeats, a draw and no goals whatsoever. If the jitters were setting in, it was incredibly bad timing.

With just four fixtures remaining, City had to rely on a scrambled own goal to edge past Sheffield Wednesday at Maine Road to finish 1-0, but the 2-0 home win four days later over Everton was far more assured. Mercer's men believed. The players believed. The fans hoped.

The trip to White Hart lane to face a Spurs team out to avenge their 4-1 thrashing at Maine Road the previous December was christened "The Ballet on Ice" by the watching media. The Blues were at their irresistible best in the first half and were 3-0 up by half-time. The trouble was that they had literally run themselves into the ground and Tottenham began to take a grip of the game, sensing an unlikely comeback.

As it was, City clung on to win 3-1 and were left with the scenario the whole of Manchester had longed and dreaded could happen in equal measure.

Both City and United would go into the last day of the season with the potential of winning the title. Liverpool had an outside chance, but it was really all about who would be crowned kings of Manchester.

City were top and in control of their own destiny but faced a tough trip to Newcastle United, who rarely lost at home. United faced Sunderland at Old Trafford.

More than 20,000 Blues made the trip to the north east to cheer their heroes on and were rewarded with an unbelievable match. Summerbee struck City ahead but the Geordies levelled almost immediately. On the half-hour, Young restored the Blues' lead, but again the home side drew level almost straight away and the teams went in at the break level at 2-2.

Back came City, with further goals from Young and Lee giving them the breathing space they desperately needed. Newcastle still pulled one back five minutes from time and came close to levelling before the whistle went for full-time to send the travelling hordes wild with delight.

City had won their first title for the first time in 31 years and the celebrations lasted long into the summer. The fact that United had lost their game against Sunderland was irrelevant – nobody was going to steal the thunder from the new champions of England.

The decision to set off on a six-week post-season tour of the USA was to prove costly for City. With the title win at Newcastle less than a week old, the team flew across the Atlantic for an exhausting nine-game tour that would last until mid-June. The fatigue of the trip meant the normal pre-season break was halved, and it would show in the 1968/69 campaign.

Whether Malcolm Allison was being his usual bullish self or whether he really believed his own words, his statement to the press that City would "terrify Europe" came back to haunt him all too quickly.

The Blues entered European competition for the first time and, as champions of England, in the biggest one of all, the European Cup. They were given a tough draw against Turkish champions Fenerbahçe. With no experience of continental football to draw upon, City struggled to break down disciplined and resolute opposition at Maine Road and the game ended 0-0. Two weeks later, City were out. Despite taking the lead with a precious away goal through Tony Coleman, City eventually lost 2-1. Inexperience, plus a difficult baptism in the competition, conspired to lead to an early exit, and domestic silverware was, once again, the main focus for the Blues.

But the champions were finding the defence of their title increasingly difficult too. By late November City had won only four of their opening 19 league games. Floundering near the foot of the table, the Blues only briefly showed glimpses of the form that had won them the Division One championship the season before.

The goals had dried up somewhat and only now and then – particularly at Maine Road – did City shift into top gear: successive home wins against West Brom (5-1) Burnley (7-0) and Chelsea (4-1). So wretched was the club's away form that they would only win twice on the road all season – at Sunderland and Manchester United.

City's annoying inconsistency had resurfaced, and the loss of skipper Tony Book with an Achilles injury proved to be a devastating blow to the Blues, although he made a miraculous recovery to once again lead the side again in the New Year.

The players targeted the FA Cup to provide welcome relief from a frustrating league season and City steamrollered toward the final with a

Left: Tony Book, captain of the title-winning 1967/68 City side.

Above: City manager Joe Mercer (left) and Dave Ewing, an FA Cup-winner in 1956, who would return to Maine Road after retiring as a player in the 1960s.

ONE LEAGUE WIN FROM THE FINAL 18 MATCHES PLACED THEM IN 11TH, AND THERE WAS ALSO A SERIOUS STRAIN IN THE MERCER-ALLISON PARTNERSHIP, WITH BIG MAL KEEN TO TAKE ON THE MANAGER'S ROLE ON HIS OWN.

Above: The famous "Ballet on Ice" game at Maine Road between City and Tottenham. Malcolm Allison told his players to go and play as though the surface was grass and to ignore the snow and ice as much as possible – it worked, too, with the Blues' sure-footed display resulting in a graceful 4-1 win.

determination and focus that had been absent from the majority of the league performances.

Luton, Newcastle and Blackburn were dispatched along the way and single-goal victories against Spurs and Everton set up a final against Leicester City, where a glorious Neil Young strike won the trophy for City for the first time in 13 years. At the end of up-and-down season Book was named joint Footballer of the Year (with Tottenham's Dave Mackay) by the Football Writers' Association for both his recovery and leadership during the second half of the campaign.

The 1969/70 season proved to be another successful one for City. The league form again paled in comparison to the Blues' prowess in cup competitions and, though City crashed out as holders of the FA Cup to Manchester United, the League Cup and European Cup Winners' Cup proved entirely different matters.

There were no major personnel changes to the side, but Tony Coleman left a few games into

the new season to begin his wanderings once again. "TC" had more than played his part in City's glorious spell and it was, perhaps, a pity that he left before he had yet more medals to add to his collection.

In defence, Tommy Booth was becoming a vital part of the back line and would play in all bar one of the league fixtures. With the lessons of Fenerbahçe learned, City entered the European Cup Winners' Cup with a steely determination to prove that coach Malcolm Allison had been right to say his men would be a force to be reckoned with in European football. A fantastic 3-3 draw away to Athletic Bilbao was followed by an equally impressive 3-0 home victory. In the League Cup, City had dispatched Southport and Liverpool. The two competitions would run in tandem all season.

By November, City had seen off Everton and QPR to line up a two-legged semi-final with United. It was to be a painful season for the Reds in derby games as City also thrashed them 4-0 in the league

in November, with Colin Bell grabbing a brace.

Belgians Lierse were dumped out 8-0 on aggregate in Europe, leaving the Blues to look forward to further action the following spring.

Back in the League Cup, United went down again at Maine Road, though the 2-1 loss meant there was work to be done in the Old Trafford return and, two weeks later, City booked an immediate return to Wembley with a 2-2 draw. The New Year saw the Blues endure a miserable 10-match run without a victory, but they would return to form in time for Europe and the League Cup final.

Paired with Portuguese outfit Académica de Coimbra, City played out a bruising 0-0 draw away in the first leg and then flew back to face West Brom at Wembley three days later. Joe Mercer described the surface for the final as "a pig of a pitch" following the Horse of the Year Show days earlier. The Blues mastered the conditions and Glyn Pardoe hit an extra-time winner as City secured a third major trophy in just three years. An incredible achievement – and there was more to come.

Tony Towers scored the only goal of the return with Académica to set up a semi-final with German side Schalke. Despite losing the first leg of the

semi-final 1-0, the Blues were at their very best on the return leg, winning 5-1 in front of an ecstatic Maine Road crowd. They would now travel to Austria to face Polish side Górnik Zabrze in the final.

The Blues had finished in 10th place in Division One by the time they walked out into a rain-sodden Vienna evening. With the majority of the 10,000 fans from Manchester, City set about the Poles, and Neil Young and Franny Lee scored the goals in a memorable 2-1 win. Tony Book again lifted another major trophy and Allison later claimed he'd been right all along about his side but had just got it a year wrong!

The City fans kept pinching themselves to believe it was all really happening. Just six years before, they had been languishing mid-table in the second tier. How quickly things had changed.

The Blues' first full season in the 1970s was also the beginning of the end of the glory years at Maine Road for some considerable time. Malcolm Allison was becoming more frustrated with his position as number two and craved the power he believed he'd been promised by Joe Mercer when the pair first teamed up.

Above: Francis Lee, No.7, celebrates putting City 4-2 up at St James' Park on the final day of the 1967/68 season. Needing to beat Newcastle United to guarantee the title, the goal proves crucial as City edge a thrilling contest 4-3 to claim only the second title in the Club's history

Above: Tommy Booth (third left) nets the last-gasp winning goal to give City a dramatic 1-0 win over Everton in the 1968/60 FA Cup semi-final at Villa Park.

Right: Manager Joe Mercer is one of the first to congratulate Mike Summerbee after the 1-0 win over Leicester City in the 1969 FA Cup final at Wembley. It was Summerbee's cross that set up Neil Young's winner.

The 1970/71 campaign began with the Blues in superb form, dropping just two points from their opening eight fixtures and conceding just three goals. It was the form of champions – but it wouldn't last.

Carlisle United ended City's interest in the League Cup they'd won just a few months earlier with a 2-1 victory at Blundell Park and the defence of the European Cup Winners' Cup almost ended in embarrassment when only the away-goals rule saw City edge past Irish minnows Linfield. Then a run of just 2 league wins in 11 matches saw Mercer's side tumbling down the table.

Honved were confidently dispatched amidst the poor league form with an excellent 1-0 win in Hungary and a 2-0 victory at Maine Road. The draw for the next round paired City with old foes Górnik Zabrze in the quarter-final. City had beaten the Polish giants to win the trophy the previous season and knew it would be a tough test in their quest to retain it, but the Blues would have to wait until March – four months away – to play them.

City could well have slipped out of the First Division, so poor were their results.

In the Cup Winners' Cup, things also looked bleak following a 2-0 defeat to Górnik in Poland, when City were outclassed on the night. But a much improved performance at Maine Road saw the team win 2-0, with goals from Ian Mellor and Mike Doyle. Bizarrely, a replay was arranged for Copenhagen but it didn't stop City's progress, with a fine 3-1 victory setting up an all-English semi-final with Chelsea.

City knew they were more capable of getting a result in London, but injury rocked them with the loss of Doyle, Heslop, Summerbee, Oakes and Bell – a devastating quintet to be absent – yet a brave performance allowed Chelsea to take only a 1-0 lead to Maine Road.

There were still several key players again absent from the second leg, which was played

in front of a crowd of almost 44,000, but it was to be a disappointing evening for the home fans, as reserve goalkeeper Ron Healey turned a cross into his own net for the only goal of the game. Chelsea went on to win the Cup, beating Real Madrid in the final.

For City, what had started out as a season full of promise had ended with bitter disappointment. One league win from the final 18 matches placed them in 11th, and there was also a serious strain in the Mercer-Allison partnership, with Big Mal keen to take on the manager's role on his own.

Despite the rumbling of discontent, Mercer was still the manager of City for the beginning of the 1971/72 season. However, by October, Malcolm Allison was effectively in charge, with Mercer becoming General Manager. On the pitch, the Blues were looking back to their best, with only two defeats in their opening 19 fixtures. Franny Lee was making the headlines for his success from the penalty spot and often won the awards with what many considered a perfect five (a score in diving). Lee shrugged off accusations and continued to score with or without penalties.

November saw a fantastic Manchester derby watched by more than 63,000 fans at Maine Road, with Summerbee scoring at the death to earn his side a share of the spoils in a thrilling 3-3 draw. Striker Wyn Davies was now leading the line for the Blues and many believed they were on their way to another league title.

Behind the scenes, Joe Mercer was becoming more and more disillusioned with his treatment by the City board. He was being treated shabbily by the chairman and directors and felt – quite rightly –

Left: A pitch invasion follows Denis Law's late winner for City at Old Trafford. The 1-0 win confirms Manchester United's relegation to Division Two.

Above: Midfielder Colin Bell was considered to be the beating heart of the Manchester City team during the Blues' glory years of the late 1960s and early 1970s.

he deserved more respect. The problem continued throughout the season.

By the middle of March, City were four points clear at the top of the table and seemingly heading for the title. For the final push, Allison signed entertainer supreme Rodney Marsh for a club-record fee of £200,000. It meant a change of style for the team, with Marsh happy to hold the ball up on the wing and sometimes slow down City's pacey counter-attacks. Whether Marsh was the reason or not, critically, it coincided with a run-in of four victories in nine matches.

City finished fourth, just a point behind champions Derby County, in the closest title race yet. Many blamed the arrival of Marsh for the disappointing finish. At least Franny Lee set a new record for penalties scored in a season – 13 – to give him an impressive tally of 33 league goals.

In June 1972, Joe Mercer left Maine Road to become General Manager at Coventry City, leaving the majority of fans disgusted at the club's handling of a man who had made their side a domestic powerhouse during his reign. What could have ended a memorable season had instead ended on a disappointing note.

Malcolm Allison's promotion to team manager seemed to rock a previously steady boat and the Blues' began season 1972/73 with five defeats in the opening six matches.

A couple of wins interspersed with two heavy away losses left Allison's side floundering near the foot of the table. Behind the scenes, Peter Swales was in the process of becoming the club's chairman after supporters had registered their anger at the shoddy treatment of Mercer.

City finally strung a run together to claw their way up the table with a run of five wins, two draws and one defeat in eight games and, by the end of the campaign, they would be grateful of the form that would be enough to keep them clear of relegation. But just three wins in the next 16 had convinced Big Mal he could no longer motivate the players and he instead left for Crystal Palace. It was the end of an era.

Johnny Hart, a star of the 1950s City side, was promoted to manager from the coaching staff, but he, too, would be forced to vacate the hot-seat. He guided the side to finish in 11th place, losing only one of the last seven league matches.

Various pressures soon took their toll on the popular Hart, but he still pulled off a major coup in the close season by picking up Scottish international Denis Law on a free transfer from United, much to the dismay of the Reds' fans. Law made an instant impact by scoring twice on his second debut for the club – having played for the Blues back in 1961 – in a 3-1 win over Birmingham. With Lee, Summerbee, Marsh and Bell, he had joined what was still, without doubt, the most exciting forward line in England.

Hart was finally forced to step down as manager in the autumn as his condition worsened and former skipper Tony Book stepped in until a new man was found. The team was inconsistent but was progressing well in the League Cup by the time Ron Saunders was appointed as the new permanent boss. Saunders had a reputation as a dour disciplinarian and, after the enigmatic Allison and charm of Mercer, he failed to establish a relationship with the players, though still helped

Above: Paul Power (arms raised) wheels away after scoring a superb free-kick in the 100th minute of the FA Cup semi-final against Ipswich Town at Villa Park.

Left: In the Centenary FA Cup final against Tottenham in 1981. Tommy Hutchison emulated Charlton's Bert Turner (1946) by scoring at both for both teams.

guide the club to the 1974 League Cup final against Wolves.

City lost 2-1 but signed Dennis Tueart and Mick Horswill from Sunderland with some of the cup-run profits. Saunders was sacked after just a few months in charge and left Maine Road shocked and angry. Peter Swales was now the new City chairman and he had shown he wasn't afraid to wield the axe if he felt things weren't right. He offered the post to Tony Book, the unanimous choice of the players, and the former captain was only too happy to take on the role.

City's season ended with a derby at Old Trafford, with United needing a win and results elsewhere going in their favour. In an unbelievable twist of irony, Law scored the only goal of the game with a cheeky backheel – his last kick in club football – and United were relegated. The Blues, meanwhile, looked forward to a new era under Book.

Tony Book's first job as new City boss was to slowly dismantle an ageing side and rebuild a new, younger team. Francis Lee was the first big name to leave the club with the crowd favourite joining Derby County. Glyn Pardoe was struggling with injury and Tommy Booth was having severe back problems, so reinforcements were needed.

Book still had Alan Oakes, Colin Bell, Mike Doyle and Mike Summerbee at the club and their

experience would be crucial as the changes were implemented. The first new arrival was Asa Hartford from West Bromwich Albion. The busy Scottish midfielder had been due to sign for Leeds but failed a medical due to a hole-in-the-heart condition.

Book had watched Hartford several times and was delighted the deal fell through! He wasted no time in bringing what would prove to be a fantastic signing for the Blues to Maine Road. He would add Geoff Hammond and Joe Royle as the season progressed, as well as blooding youngsters Peter Barnes and Ged Keegan.

Franny Lee had made a dramatic return to Maine Road with a spectacular strike that helped his new club, Derby, to a 2-1 win. He was overjoyed at the goal and many felt he ran to the Platt Lane Stand to celebrate out of habit!

Dennis Tueart was exciting the City fans with his dynamic runs on the wing and he scored his first of many hat-tricks for the Blues against his hometown club, Newcastle United, in a 5-1 home victory in January. Colin Bell revelled in having more opportunities to get in striking positions since Lee's departure and finished the season with 15 league goals – his best haul to date.

Royle's arrival from Everton had given Book's side a much needed target man and the Blues were already beginning to look like a team capable of challenging for major honours once again. They finished the season in eighth position, but more silverware was just around the corner...

The changing of the guard continued under Book, with strapping centre-half Dave Watson added to the squad, while Mike Summerbee ended his glorious time at Maine Road to join Burnley and Rodney Marsh was transferred to Tampa Bay Rowdies amidst much controversy. Colin Bell had been lost to a crippling knee injury in a League Cup tie against United, but the Blues went on to win the 1976 League Cup with a wonder-goal from Tueart against Newcastle United. Youngsters Kenny

Clements, Gary Owen and Peter Barnes were exciting emerging talents coming through.

There were more changes for the 1976/77 campaign, with Brian Kidd and Jimmy Conway joining Book's side, and long-serving defender Alan Oakes leaving the club after 18 years. Paul Power was yet another promising youngster who was making a name for himself as City prepared an all-out assault on the league title.

The Blues began with only 2 defeats in their first 25 games, with Joe Corrigan and his defenders keeping 13 clean sheets. UEFA Cup interest had ended in the first round against Juventus, and Aston Villa and Leeds had been responsible for domestic departures from cup competitions. With only the league to concentrate on, it was Liverpool and the Blues neck and neck on the run-in. City suffered a few crushing blows. United completed the double over Book's men at Old Trafford and, in April, Liverpool beat City 2-1 at Anfield. Worse was to come as Derby thrashed City 4-0 and both Villa and Everton took a point off City in the games that remained. By the end, Liverpool had won the league by a single point and the Blues were left to rue missed opportunities during what had been an excellent league programme.

Mike Channon was the only notable close-season purchase for the start of 1977/78, moving from Southampton for a record fee of £300,000. City were again consistent but were, once more, knocked out of the UEFA Cup at the first hurdle. Despite leading 2-0 with 10 minutes left against Poles Widzew Lódz, the game ended 2-2 and a 0-0 draw in Poland sent Book's men out on away goals. In the league, things were much brighter and City were again challenging strongly. City were again challenging strongly. Dennis Tueart completed his third hat-trick of the season, sending Newcastle packing 4-0 on Boxing Day – the day Colin Bell made an emotional return to first-team football after an agonizing fight to save his career.

The win over the Magpies was the first of seven successive league victories, keeping the pressure on Brian Clough's Nottingham Forest, but the gap would never be closed and City – now without a New York Cosmos-bound Tueart – finished in fourth. The highlight of a largely disappointing 1978/79 season was the arrival of Polish World Cup captain Kaziu Deyna and a terrific run in the UEFA Cup. City beat FC Twente and Standard Liège to win a plum tie with Italian giants AC Milan. The first game in Italy was postponed due to fog but rearranged for the following afternoon. The Blues raced into a 2-0 lead, with Paul Power scoring an amazing solo goal, but the tie ended 2-2. The second leg found the Blues in imperious form and goals from Kidd, Booth and Hartford gave them a 3-0 lead at the break. There were no more goals and City headed into the quarterfinals to face German outfit Borussia Mönchengladbach, where they would lose 4-2 on aggregate.

Deyna showed only glimpses of the brilliance that had made him a legend in his homeland but his skills were, on occasion, a joy to watch. Meanwhile, concerned at the Blues' dip in fortunes, Swales decided there was only one man who could help turn things around. By the start of 1979, Malcolm Allison was back at Maine Road as coach – a move that was warmly greeted by the majority of City fans. Dennis Tueart returned from New York Cosmos two-thirds of the way through the programme, but a humiliating loss to Shrewsbury

Above: Malcolm Allison's ill-fated return to City as team manager proved the old adage "you should never go back" to be true. Tony Book took on a more general role, but the decision to sell many established stars and replace them with youngsters and little-known players proved flawed.

Town in the FA Cup and a finish of 15th saw Allison take command and the loyal Book side-lined.

It was the dawn of a turbulent run for City, which would take more than a decade to recover from.

The first full season of the 1980s would be unforgettable for City fans for all the wrong reasons. Big Mal was clinging on to his job for dear life and really should probably have been replaced in the summer, but such was his almost hypnotic hold on chairman Peter Swales and the board that he earned at least one more crack at revitalizing the team.

It wasn't that he'd lost his talent as a coach – the ability he had on the training ground was never in doubt – it was more to do with the lack of a steadying Joe Mercer alongside him. He was steering a sinking ship into deeper waters and was, in effect, the master of his own downfall, replacing internationals such as Dave Watson, Asa Hartford, Brian Kidd, Gary Owen and Peter Barnes with the likes of Steve Daley, Paul Sugrue and Barry Silkman, who simply weren't good enough.

The first dozen games of the 1980/81 season were painful for all concerned. City fans had to endure some terrible football before Swales did the decent thing and relieved Allison of his position. Four draws and seven defeats in and City were anchored to the foot of the table headed for Division Two football. Swales looked for a new manager with personality and character big enough to save his club and build a brighter future. Enter Norwich City

boss John Bond; every bit the flamboyant larger-than-life character Swales felt was needed to erase the memory of a painful couple of years. Bond quit Carrow Road and headed north to take up the reigns of a club teetering on the brink.

Bond watched from the stands as his new club went down to a last-minute Archie Gemmill penalty against Birmingham, which proved to be the only goal of the game. He gave teenager Gary Buckley his debut, feeling width was needed for his side, and City played with style to win their first game of the season 3-1. The first two games had shown Bond where the deficiencies lay and he immediately signed three Scottish veterans for a total outlay of under £500,000. Midfield warrior Gerry Gow was drafted from Bristol City, and attacking full-back Bobby McDonald and classy winger Tommy Hutchison both arrived from Coventry City.

From there on in, the Blues were a different team. They steadily climbed away from the foot of the table with a series of impressive wins and made progress in both domestic cup competitions. For the League Cup, Bond's new signings were cup-tied so he was basically playing the same team Allison had been putting out before he was sacked and, for a while, it seemed as though there were two teams at Maine Road, both playing equally well. City reached the semi-final of the League Cup but went out controversially to Liverpool 2-1 over two legs, with at least one unbelievably bad refereeing decision robbing the

Blues of a vital first-leg goal.

In the FA Cup, the 100th edition of the competition, there were a series of ironic pairings, first with Crystal Palace – Allison's new team – and then Norwich City – Bond's old team – in rounds three and four. Both were easily dispatched 4-0 and 6-0, respectively. A Tommy Booth header saw off the challenge of Fourth Division Peterborough at London Road in the last 16 and then an epic tussle with Everton – 2-2 at Goodison and then 3-1 at Maine Road – eased City into the semi-finals, where they faced Bobby Robson's buoyant Ipswich Town at Villa Park.

It was an unforgettable day for City fans as the Blues won 1-0 with a glorious Paul Power free-kick in the 100th minute of the semi-final. Many supporters would later say they enjoyed the semi-final even more than the final and, given what came next, it isn't hard to understand why. Surely City's name was on the trophy? All the irony and victories against the odds suggested it must be.

Thousands of City fans queued at Maine Road for hours to buy their cup-final tickets as excitement reached fever pitch in the blue half of Manchester, but there were nowhere near enough tickets to meet the demand. With a comfortable mid-table league position secured, the Blues walked out with Tottenham onto the lush Wembley turf for the FA Cup Final. The game ended 1-1 after Tommy Hutchison put City ahead and then bizarrely deflected a Glenn Hoddle free-kick past Joe Corrigan for a late own goal. City still had chances to win the match in extra time, but it wasn't to be.

The Wembley replay five days later was one of the most exciting witnessed at the old stadium. Despite a stunning equalizing goal from teenager Steve McKenzie, and leading 2-1 with 20 minutes to go, the Blues lost 3-2, after a wonderful solo winning goal from Ricardo Villa. The dream was over, and the omens were wrong. It wasn't a storybook ending the fairy-tale season had demanded after all.

Bond's second campaign in the hot-seat, for a time, looked as if it may be even more exciting, especially when England striker Trevor Francis was signed from Nottingham Forest for £1.2 million. Francis was one of the best strikers in the country and his debut away to Stoke attracted a 10,000-strong travelling army of Blues supporters desperate to see him play – and he didn't disappoint the Mancunian hordes, scoring twice in a 3-1 win.

Four weeks later – and just as Dennis Tueart had done 18 months earlier – another former hero re-signed for the Blues. Asa Hartford, one of the big-name casualties of Malcolm Allison's purge, had never wanted to leave City in the first place and the midfielder was happy to return. The manager then signed his son, Kevin, from Seattle Sounders to bolster the defence. By Christmas, the Blues were challenging at the top of the table and a fantastic display at Anfield on Boxing Day gave Bond's men a 3-1 win – their first victory away to Liverpool for almost three decades. Two days later and the Blues went top with a 2-1 win over Wolves, but they could not maintain their challenge and, like a horse that heads the pack too soon, the Blues fell away dramatically with just 5 more wins from the final 22 games.

Bond's magic seemed to be fading, as was his infectious enthusiasm, and the surge of optimism that had perhaps papered over the cracks somewhat during his first 18 months in charge was gone.

Left: Franny Lee attacks the Manchester United defence during an Old Trafford derby.

Above: Francis Lee – Joe Mercer called him "the missing piece of the jigsaw".

Left: The City team which would win promotion in 1965/66 line up for a team photo at Maine Road.

Below: City's "Holy Trinity" of (left to right) Mike Summerbee, Francis Lee and Colin Bell.

IN AN UNBELIEVABLE TWIST OF IRONY, LAW
SCORED THE ONLY GOAL OF THE GAME WITH
A CHEEKY BACKHEEL – HIS LAST KICK IN CLUB
FOOTBALL – AND UNITED WERE RELEGATED.

Above: Best of friends – off the pitch! Manchester United legend George Best and Mike Summerbee outside their Manchester city-centre fashion shop "Edwardia".

Left: Malcolm Allison celebrates with the City fans at Wembley with the League Cup trophy after the 2-1 extra time win over West Bromwich Albion.

Below: The elegant Neil Young – a forward blessed with technique and a devastating left-foot. He scored the 1969 FA Cup final winner against Leicester City.

Right: Combative Scottish midfielder Gerry Gow, signed from Bristol City in 1981, he became a huge crowd favourite with the City fans.

Above top: Rodney Marsh challenges Tottenham's Pat Jennings at Maine Road.

Above: Former Poland captain Kaziu Deyna in action for City against Arsenal.

Right: Mercurial winger Tony Coleman, one of the stars of the late 1960s City team.

Left: Skipper Tony Book is presented with the 1970 European Cup Winners' Cup after a 2-1 win over Gornik in Vienna. Despite torrential rain, the Blues win their first European trophy.

Below: Dennis Tueart attempts an acrobatic overhead kick against Coventry City.

Right: Club legend Colin Bell poses for a preseason photo – complete with holiday sandals! In the background, work continues on the new North Stand.

Left: One of Manchester City's greatest servants as player, manager, coach and Life President – Tony Book.

Below left: John Bond, the manager who helped transform a relegation-bound City team into FA Cup finalists, League Cup semi-finalists and a comfortable mid-table finish in 1980/81.

Above: Malcolm Allison (left) and Joe Mercer – coach and manager – a partnership that many believe to have been the best the Club has ever had. Together, they won the League title, FA Cup, League Cup and European Cup Winners' Cup between 1968 and 1970.

LEE WAS TOP SCORER AGAIN IN 1970/71 HAD HIS BEST SEASON FOR THE CLUB IN 1971/72, SCORING AN INCREDIBLE 35 GOALS IN 46 LEAGUE AND CUP GAMES AS CITY ALMOST WON THE LEAGUE TITLE; SADLY "ALMOST" DOESN'T WIN MEDALS OR TROPHIES.

COLIN BELL

When Malcolm Allison sat in the stand at Gigg Lane loudly expressing his doubts over Colin Bell's ability, he was, of course, attempting to convince the other watching managers and scouts that they were wasting their time watching the young Bury midfielder.

"He can't pass it, he can't tackle and he's no good in the air," he said, ensuring ears around him heard everything he was saying. Allison's plan seemed to work, as he seemingly managed to delay any firm bids and snapped up Bell once City had raised the cash to buy him.

Wearing the No.10 shirt, he made his debut in a 2-1 win at Derby and scored one of the goals. He played in all 11 remaining games and City didn't lose a match, picking up the Division Two championship for good measure. The midfielder had already made an impact, but there was so much more to come.

Bell was an ever-present during his first full season and finished top scorer with a dozen goals as the Blues limped to a final placing of 15th in the table in a campaign of consolidation.

Francis Lee joined the club partway through the 1967/68 season and, for many, this represented the final piece of the Mercer-Allison blueprint. City went on to win the league title, with Bell inspirational throughout the campaign. The fans loved his seemingly limitless stamina, drive and all-round contribution to the team. He was the beating heart of the Manchester City team of the late 1960s and early 1970s and, along with Lee and Mike Summerbee, formed the legendary "Holy Trinity" of players who would inspire the club to as yet uncharted heights.

A fantastic footballer on the pitch, Bell was a quiet man off it, never seeking adulation or headlines, even though he'd more than earned them.

While Summerbee, Lee and Doyle would wind up the opposition, the press and opposing fans, Bell quietly ticked along in the background, painfully shy, preferring to let his feet do the talking.

United had George Best, City had Colin Bell.

As the years ticked by, Bell's influence seemed to grow stronger rather than fade and, while the press and pundits claimed Rodney Marsh's signing cost City the 1971/72 league title, few noted that Colin bell had missed nine games through injury, during which time the Blues won just four times.

Sadly – and with Bell still at his peak – he suffered a horrible knee injury in a League Cup tie with Manchester United at Maine Road. Bell, attacking the Platt Lane end of the ground, was caught in two minds as to what to do as he approached Martin Buchan on the edge of the Reds' box. He opted to cut inside instead of glide past on the right and was scythed down by the United man.

Undoubtedly, it was the beginning of the end for Bell, though he did come back later that season and was again on the end of a nasty challenge, this time from Ray Kennedy as the Blues beat Arsenal 3-1 at Maine Road – that injury was, many believed, as bad as the one against United and he was side-lined for the next 18 months, doing everything he possibly could do work his way back to fitness.

Quietly and stoically, he pounded the streets around Maine Road as some mobility returned before he was finally passed fit to begin training again.

He made an emotional comeback against Newcastle United as a second-half sub on Boxing Day 1977 and received one of the most emotional ovations ever witnessed at Maine Road. His appearance galvanized his team-mates and the crowd, and City scored four goals to win the game. He played sporadically after that but, understandably, he was never the same again. His bravery, though, was admired by all in football and, at City, the man was – and still is – a god.

Finally, the pain and heartache of never being able to move fluidly on a pitch again forced his retirement.

BELL, COLIN
1966–79

APPEARANCES
489 (+3 as sub)

GOALS
152

POSITION
Attacking midfielder

BORN
Hesleden, Co. Durham

Right: Colin Bell – regarded as one of the best players City have ever had. Injury prematurely ended a wonderful career for club and country.

MIKE SUMMERBEE

Joe Mercer's decision to make Mike Summerbee his first signing as Manchester City manager prior to the 1965/66 season was inspired. The winger arrived for just £31,000 from Swindon Town, upping his weekly wage from £35 to £40.

The Swindon board had been reluctant to let their rising star leave the County Ground, but economics demanded they cashed in and ultimately sold to the highest bidder, and fortunately for the Blues, that was Mercer, who had played football with Mike's dad, George, during the Second World War.

Summerbee proved an instant hit with the City fans and fitted perfectly into a side destined for promotion from the Second Division. He played in all 52 games in league and cup competitions, scoring 10 goals as the Blues returned to the top flight after a 3-year absence. He added a new dimension to the team with his trickery and ability to get to the bye-line and whip over wonderful crosses. He was also one of the first wingers to "defend from the front" – tackling back and offering 50-50 balls in order to give the full-back an early taste of what was to come. Franny Lee said some years later that it was a form of "retaliating first"!

Defenders knew they'd been in a battle when up against Summerbee and, along with Tony Coleman, Lee and Neil Young City, were a formidable attacking force who helped power City to the 1967/68 Division One title. Summerbee's contribution was substantial that season, playing 50 games in all competitions and scoring 19 goals – a fantastic return. Mike "Buzzer" Summerbee scored the opening goal on the final day away to Newcastle to help secure the title and he laid on a perfect cross for Neil Young to hammer home the only goal of the 1969 FA Cup final.

But it wasn't just about the football. The fans loved Buzzer because he was a real character who played the game in the right spirit. He was always prepared to enjoy himself – often with a deadpan look on his face – and would play to the crowd on many occasions, throwing snowballs, sitting on the ball, blowing his nose on the corner flag away to Manchester United – there were dozens of memorable moments.

Buzzer ended being big pals with United's George Best. The pair even opened a boutique together at one point and George was best man on Buzzer's wedding day.

Summerbee thoroughly enjoyed the life of a footballer and was a regular member of the first team for eight seasons, although he played more as an out-and-out winger as time went on. Like many City stars of the era and since, his haul of eight England caps was scant reward for his consistency and performances at club level, which merited many more.

He was also instrumental in the 2-1 League Cup final win over West Brom a year later, but sustained a hairline fracture of the leg during the game, which meant he missed the European Cup Winners' Cup final just seven weeks later. Buzzer continued to give excellent service for many years at Maine Road, becoming skipper for the 1973/74 season and leading his team out at Wembley for the 1974 League Cup final against Wolves, although he had to settle for a runners-up medal on the day.

When Tony Book became manager in 1974, he had the difficult job of dismantling an ageing side full of former team-mates, Summerbee included, and when Burnley lodged a bid of £25,000 and his time with City was at an end – at least until he returned as the club's ambassador in 2009.

SUMMERBEE, MIKE
1965–75
APPEARANCES
443
GOALS
67
POSITION
Winger
BORN
Preston

Left: Mike Summerbee – a born winner, skilful winger and entertainer who was integral to the Mercer/Allison team and enjoyed a decade at the top with City.

FRANCIS LEE

Francis "Franny" Lee joined City in 1967 from Bolton Wanderers for a fee £60,000. Though only 23, Lee had been playing senior football for seven years and he slotted in perfectly to the football and team ethic Joe Mercer and Malcolm Allison wanted in their side. It wasn't too long before the management and supporters realized that the Westhoughton lad was the final piece of the Blues' jigsaw.

Lee, though physically short and stocky in appearance, was guaranteed to give any defender a difficult 90 minutes, no matter what their size – in fact, the bigger the better. Feisty and fiery, he backed up guts with skill and intelligence and his impact was immediate.

The Blues won eight and drew three of Lee's first 11 league games and he scored eight goals as City sailed toward the summit of the table. Franny quickly volunteered to take penalties for the team and would go on to win the majority of them!

By the time City lifted the championship in May 1968, Lee had scored 16 goals in 31 games and it was his strike at St James' Park on the final day of the season that effectively won the game and the title for Mercer's men.

Bell, Lee and Summerbee became known as the "Holy Trinity" and the trio inspired more success the following year with an FA Cup final triumph over Leicester. Lee finished joint top scorer in the league.

There was a cup double for the Blues in 1970 as they first lifted the League Cup and then the European Cup Winners' Cup. Lee scored the decisive goal in Vienna (from the spot, of course) to secure a 2-1 win over Poland's Górnik Zabrze and a first major European trophy for the club – that £60,000 was beginning to look like a bargain for City.

Lee finished top scorer again in 1970/71 and had his most prolific season for the club in 1971/72 when they almost won another league title – but almost doesn't win medals or trophies, unfortunately. Lee scored an incredible 35 goals in 46 league and cup games and converted a record 15 penalties along the way.

Off the field, Lee's sharp business acumen ensured he was well on his way to becoming a millionaire while still a very young man, and he was also an England regular, starting in three matches for his country at the 1970 World Cup finals in Mexico. In all, he scored 10 goals in 27 appearances for the national team.

In 1972/73, the unorthodox forward was becoming restless at Maine Road and, despite finishing joint top scorer for the Blues again with his third total of 14 league goals in six seasons, the managerial upheavals that had seen Mercer moved unceremoniously "upstairs" and then Allison quit after less than a year in charge left him wondering about his future at Maine Road. Johnny Hart, Ron Saunders and then Tony Book all took turns in managing the club, meaning that, after having just one manager for seven years, City had now had five in the space of two.

Three days before the start of the new season, Derby County offered £100,000 for Lee's services and Tony Book didn't stand in his way.

It was a wonderful move for the ex-City forward and for the Rams and, just as he had done in his first season with City, Lee was inspirational as Derby went on to lift the league championship in 1974/75.

He played on for one more season at the Baseball Ground before retiring to concentrate on his thriving wastepaper business and successful racehorse stable. He would return to become chairman of City in the mid-1990s.

LEE, FRANCIS
1967–74

APPEARANCES
330

GOALS
148

POSITION
Forward

BORN
Westhoughton, Bolton

Right: Brash, brave and talented – Francis Lee arrived from Bolton with a swagger and confidence that was infectious.

4. 1982–1998: TROUBLED TIMES

Trevor Francis was sold to Sampdoria after just one season at Maine Road and some even suggested the smart new roof on the Main Stand was the reason that City sold their crown jewel – all denied by chairman Swales, of course, who was regularly in the headlines for one reason or another. Only Bobby McDonald remained from the famed tartan trio (Gerry Gow and Tommy Hutchison were the others) and the players coming in were, in general, an odd assortment of bargain-basement journeymen and lower-league unknowns.

The writing was on the wall for all to see – City were sinking fast and a 4-0 thrashing in the FA Cup 4th round at Brighton in January 1983 was the final straw for Bond, who promptly resigned. His assistant, John Benson, was promoted to manager and, subsequently, City slipped toward the relegation trapdoor in freefall. The final match of the season was at home to Luton Town, who needed a win to stay up, while a point was enough to keep City up. For 86 unbearable minutes, it appeared as though 0-0 would be enough but, as the ball came to substitute Raddy Antić on the edge of the box, the future of Manchester City was about to take a dramatic change. Antić shot low and hard past Alex Williams for what would be the only goal of the game. City were down and David Pleat's victory jig was not what more than 42,000 mortified supporters wanted to see. Some even spilled on to pitch, sending Pleat scurrying back down the tunnel to safety.

So began the real misery of the 1980s. Former Celtic manager, captain and Lisbon Lion Billy McNeill was installed as new boss for the 1983/84 season but, with little or no budget to buy reinforcements, he couldn't inspire an instant return, with City finishing in fourth position. However, there was definite progress

the following year and, for the final game of the 1984/85 campaign, a win would be enough to send the club back to the top division. Charlton Athletic were the visitors and more than 47,000 crammed into a sun-drenched Maine Road for one of the stadium's most memorable matches. For once, things went to plan and City were 2-0 up at the break, but few believed the game was over – the Blues never seemed to take the easy option on such occasions! This time, however, they followed the script to perfection and did just that with three more goals before an hour had even been played, eventually winning 5-1. Promotion had been achieved, but McNeill knew the club was in no real position to strengthen the squad and a difficult return to top-flight football ended safely in 16th position. A trip to Wembley lightened the mood, with City and Chelsea walking out at Wembley for the much-maligned Full Members' Cup final. Both teams served up a thrilling match, with the Londoners winning 5-4 – despite City scoring three goals in the dying minutes. A crowd in excess of 68,000 – around half from Manchester – enjoyed a great day out.

A few weeks later and the Blues, at last, had silverware on the sideboard again as City beat United 2-0 in the second leg of the FA Youth Cup final at Maine Road after the first leg had ended 1-1 at Old Trafford. More than 18,000 watched the second leg with an exciting crop of youngsters emerging along the way. David White, Andy Hinchcliffe, Ian Brightwell, Paul Moulden, Steve Redmond, Ian Scott and Paul Lake all looked ready to push on to the first team and their emergence couldn't have been timed any better with the Blues in serious financial trouble.

The dark clouds returned to Maine Road seven games into the 1986/87 season when Billy McNeill quit to become Aston Villa boss. Like Bond before him, he could see what was coming and didn't want to be around when it did. His assistant –

Left: Paul Lake (left) is the first to congratulate Ian Bishop after his diving header had put City 3-0 up against Manchester United in September 1989. The Blues go on to thrash the Reds 5-1 at Maine Road.

former Oldham Athletic manager Jimmy Frizzell – took over but it was a thankless task and he couldn't stop the inevitable relegation and once again, the Blues faced life in the second tier.

For the third time in his controversial role as chairman, Peter Swales turned to the manager of Norwich City to revive the Blues. This time, it was the quietly spoken Mel Machin, respected in the game as one of the most promising coaches of the time and with a solid track record of bringing young players through. With Imre Varadi and Paul Stewart leading the line, there were plenty of goals in his first season (1987/88), including an unforgettable 10-1 win over Huddersfield Town at Maine Road, but the finish of ninth was still disappointing. Reaching the quarter-finals of both the FA Cup and League Cup suggested better times lay ahead for City's young team.

Consistency during the 1988/89 season meant that, for the third time during the 1980s, the Blues' fate rested on the last game of the season. City needed a point at Bradford City and, as ever, put the travelling blue army through the mixer for the majority of the game. With four minutes left, City trailed 1-0. Then David White broke down the left and whipped in a low cross that was poked home by Trevor Morley to send the City fans delirious. City were back in the top division where they belonged. But the fans again wondered one thing: for how long this time?

The City fans' inflatable banana craze, which had peaked during 1988/89, was slowly on

the decline as manager Mel Machin began to strengthen his team in the close season of 1989 by signing Bournemouth midfielder Ian Bishop for £700,000. Bishop had inspired his old side to almost wreck City's promotion hopes in the penultimate game of the previous campaign by coming back from 3-0 down to draw 3-3 and leaving the Blues still needing a point from their final game at Bradford.

Also brought on board, for £1.1 million, was Bordeaux striker Clive Allen, who had earned a reputation as one of the best finishers since legendary Spurs striker Jimmy Greaves. It would be Allen's first goal against QPR that would give his new club their first win since returning to Division One some five games into the new programme. A couple of games later and Manchester United were back at Maine Road for the first time since 1986 for the eagerly awaited local derby. Both sides were struggling near the foot of the table and needed a morale-boosting win, but there was little clue prior to the match of the dramatic events that would give City fans a day never to forget.

The Blues were simply irresistible from start to finish and, by the time the referee blew for full-time, City had beaten United 5-1 – the biggest win over the Reds for decades. It was an unbelievable result and one some thought may even cost new United manager Alex Ferguson his job – but we all know the answer to that one! Boss Machin must have thought he had a job for life and the freedom

of the city, but football can be a particularly cruel sport and, just six league games later, following a 6-0 mauling by Derby County, Machin was axed. At the time, Peter Swales claimed Machin had no rapport with the fans – a case of the pot calling the kettle black, perhaps? – but whatever the reason, it seemed cruel on a manager who had given the supporters some local pride again.

In between managers, Colin Hendry was signed from Blackburn Rovers for £700,000 but one point from the next 12 increased pressure on Swales to find a new boss and, by mid-December, they believed they had found the right man. Howard Kendall agreed to take over the wobbling Blues after Joe Royle had turned down Swales' approach, and the new man immediately began dismantling Machin's youthful side. Experienced battlers such as Peter Reid, who became player/coach, and Alan Harper were signed and, by Christmas, crowd favourites Bishop and Trevor Morley were on their way out. Mark Ward, Adrian Heath, Gary Megson and Wayne Clarke were also brought in and, for a while, it seemed as if ex-Toffees boss Kendall wanted only ex-Everton

players. He did, of course, want players he knew and trusted and, with not much money available, was forced to take free transfers and bargain buys.

Flair and imagination were replaced by grit and determination and City steadily climbed to safety, with Arsenal striker Niall Quinn joining toward the end of the season. Fourteenth spot was a job well done by the new management team, who now drew plans for the 1990/91 season, bringing in Watford goalkeeper Tony Coton and full-back Neil Pointon. The popular Quinn was to soon forge a formidable partnership with David White and City began the new campaign impressively, losing only one of the first 11 games but also suffering the devastating loss of the hugely talented Paul Lake with a knee injury that would effectively be the beginning of the end for a player who seemed to have had the world at his feet.

Then, completely out of the blue, Kendall quit his post to return to Goodison Park, stating that "City had been an affair, but Everton was a marriage". This time, Swales did not have to look too far for the new man as a wave of fan pressure made Peter Reid the only candidate for the job. He took to

Above: David Phillips scores a vital early goal for City against Charlton Athletic on the final day of the 1984/85 campaign. Needing a win to guarantee promotion, Paul Simpson set up Phillips to score from close range and the Blues never look back, going on to win 5-1 and secure a place back in the top flight.

Above: Scottish midfield schemer Neil McNab would be voted MCFC Player of the Year twice during his seven-year stay at Maine Road.

Top right: David Phillips in action as City take on Oxford United at The Manor Ground.

his new role like the proverbial duck to water and steered City to finish in fifth place – above United for the first time since the late 1970s. Keith Curle and Steve McMahon were significant recruits during 1991/92 and again the Blues finished in fifth as the threat of stability loomed large over Maine Road! What could possibly go wrong?

Things began to go awry for Reid in the next season despite the capture of Republic of Ireland defender Terry Phelan. Tottenham's hoodoo over City that season played a significant spoiling role as the Londoners did the league double and knocked the Blues out of both cup competitions with the FA Cup defeat at Maine Road. Worse still, United won the league title and there seemed no escape for City supporters from the jubilant Reds fans that were only too happy to twist the knife.

The football had been a little stale and a finish of ninth was a definite backward step for Reid's

side. Pressure was also reaching unprecedented levels for chairman Swales too, with supporter movements aimed at ending his controversial 20-year reign – especially when a few games into the 1993/94 season, Reid was sacked. Former journalist John Maddock had been brought in initially as a PR officer and then was quickly elevated to the role of general manager. He made it clear he was no puppet and claimed he could hire and fire as he wished. Few believed this to be anything other than a Swales ploy to deflect criticism of any imminent actions. Sure enough, though, days later, Reid and his assistant, Sam Ellis, were dismissed. The City fans were disgusted and the thirst to have Swales removed reached fever pitch.

Maddock was soon busying himself seeking a replacement for Reid. Many top names were mentioned, but when the new man was announced, it was a case of "who"? Former Oxford United manager Brian Horton was unveiled as City's new manager and there was disbelief and anger among fans that a bigger name hadn't been employed. Somewhere amidst all the madness, however, Horton emerged not as the culprit but rather as somebody caught up in the middle of a circus sideshow. It was still Swales the fans wanted to go and a campaign to remove him from Maine Road seemed to be gathering momentum.

If Horton and assistant David Moss were worried how the supporters would react to their arrival, they needn't have and were warmly welcomed for their first game at Swindon. A 3-1 win eased some of the misery but, away from the field of play, events were about to take a dramatic turn for the better as far as the fans were concerned.

Francis Lee – self-made multi-millionaire businessman and one of the greatest players to have ever pulled on a sky-blue jersey – was preparing a bid to take over the club. For City fans, it was manna from heaven. Who better to save their beloved club than a former hero? A long and

sometimes painful campaign to install Lee and his consortium to power ensued until, finally, on 29 November 1993, Peter Swales quit as chairman after 20 years in the seat, paving the way for Francis Lee to assume the mantle for himself. It had been a particularly fraught and bitter period in the club's history and especially so for Swales, a man whose love for City eventually proved his own undoing.

Meanwhile, Horton was desperately trying to keep the Blues a top-flight club and the signing of David Rocastle proved to be an inspired one. With Lee now officially installed as chairman, many wondered how long the likeable Horton would keep his job for, but towards the end of the season, Peter Beagrie, Paul Walsh and Uwe Rösler were signed in time for the remaining 10 games or so and their significant contributions eased City away from the drop zone, bringing energy and zip to the forward line. For Maine Road's most famous stand – the Kippax – it was also the end of an era. A 2-2 draw with Chelsea was the last time City fans would stand on this much loved old terrace before the developers moved in to build a new all-seater stand.

With a severely reduced capacity of initially around 21,000, City entered the 1994/95 season with Brian Horton still manager. Maine Road was to witness several thrilling home games, such as a 5-2 win over Tottenham and a 3-3 draw with Southampton. The team, which now included Mike

Summerbee's son, Nicky, and in December 1994, German maverick midfielder Maurizio Gaudino, were playing exciting, attacking football. The Blues were still near the wrong end of the table and, for all the goals and entertainment, City finished 17th that season with a 3-2 home loss to QPR to be Horton's last game in charge.

Lee sacked him a few days after the QPR game and many felt he'd always been on borrowed time due to the circumstances of his arrival and subsequent events in-between. He had at least won the respect of the fans and left with his head held high.

City were making the headlines once more with activities away from the playing field and – yet again – speculation was rife as to who would become the new Maine man. And with Francis Lee in control, a big name was not only expected, it was demanded.

Several weeks passed with no new manager appointment before it was announced at the end of June that Alan Ball was to be the Blues' new boss. It seemed an odd choice given Ball's largely unsuccessful track record in management, but he was the man Francis Lee believed would take the Club forward.

Two weeks after Ball's arrival, City beat off a host of top European clubs to sign Georgian midfielder Gio Kinkladze. "Kinky" had apparently

Above: Trevor Francis makes his City debut away to Stoke City in September 1981. Tracking him, right, is former City captain Mike Doyle. An estimated 10,000 City fans made the trip to the Victoria Ground to see Francis net twice in a 3-1 victory.

Above left: Georgian playmaker Gio Kinkladze celebrates a goal during the very disappointing 1995/96 season. His skill and trickery lit up a difficult campaign.

Above right: Former England midfielder Alan Ball was City manager for just over a season, with the Blues relegated in May 1996

been on the club's wanted list for some time and Ball said shortly after the signing, "He'll have them hanging from the rafters at Maine Road to watch him play." He would be proved correct.

Also signed were Kit Symons and Eike Immel, and the opening-day draw with Tottenham suggested a promising season lay ahead, particularly with Kinkladze's sparkling debut. What followed was nothing short of disastrous – eight successive league defeats and City firmly rooted to the foot of the Premier League. A home draw with Leeds temporarily halted the run but successive League Cup and league trips to Liverpool within the space of three days intensified the gloom. The cup tie ended 4-0 to the Reds and the league match was even worse, with City thrashed 6-0. Ball infuriated City fans by later claiming that he'd "enjoyed the Liverpool display". Many thought it would be his last match in charge but, incredibly, it wasn't.

In a complete turnaround, largely inspired by the new crowd idol, Kinkladze, City enjoyed an excellent November and Ball picked up the Manager of the Month award! From one extreme to the other! By the end of January, City were still involved in the relegation scramble but had reached the FA Cup fifth round, where a draw away to United awaited them. Many felt Ball's men could

go all the way to Wembley and the game began brightly for the Blues when Rösler lobbed them into a first-half lead to send the City fans wild – maybe there was a silver lining this season? United, however, came back to win 2-1 with the help of at least one dubious refereeing decision. A week later and leaders Newcastle arrived at Maine Road, and despite the previous week's result, the Blues put on a thrilling performance and were a shade unlucky to only take a point out of a 3-3 draw.

The final home game of the season was against Liverpool. City lay third bottom and needed to better Southampton or Coventry's result to stay up. The visitors opened up a 2-0 lead without playing particularly well, but the Blues fought back with 2 goals in 8 minutes, making it 2-2 with 10 minutes or so remaining. In the dying moments, misinformation that a point was good enough resulted in City midfielder Steve Lomas attempting to waste time near the corner flag, until the message was relayed that a win, not a draw, was needed. Sadly, this summed up City's season to a tee and the final whistle blew shortly after with news filtering through that Coventry and Southampton had also drawn – and the Blues were relegated.

A summer of discontent followed with Ball allowed to continue as manager. Flitcroft, Coton, Phelan, Quinn and Curle were sold as part of a

wage-trimming exercise and the weakened Blues began life in Division One with a 1-0 win over Ipswich Town. But defeats at Bolton and then Stoke, where both home and away fans chanted for Ball to quit, indeed, signalled the end of a dismal year at the helm for Ball. His last act as boss had been to sign Paul Dickov and, ironically, it was also one of his best. The former Arsenal man would repay the £800,000 fee many times over in the next six years.

What followed was one managerial error after another. Asa Hartford valiantly filled the void until Steve Coppell was installed. He lasted exactly one month and was replaced by his assistant, Phil Neal, who lasted six weeks before Frank Clark finally became boss in December 1996. He steered City away from a second successive relegation and to a comfortable mid-table position culminating in a final home game win over Reading. The game itself wasn't memorable but the reception for Kinkladze at the end certainly was. The Georgian maestro had sacrificed a move to a number of top European clubs in order to stay and help City regain their top-flight status.

The whole of Maine Road stayed to clap the players as usual for the final home game, but the Georgian flags, banners and songs chanted throughout the game – that Kinky had ironically

missed through injury – were all pleading him not to leave. He looked taken back as he walked around the pitch in his suit and overwhelmed by the adulation. Perhaps too loyal to those who worshipped him, he decided to stay and try to help the club back to the Premier League one last time, but it was a mistake that would take his career down a far less glittering path than it surely deserved.

Clark started the 1997/98 season in charge, but he would not see it out. Another incredible chapter was written in the history of Manchester City as Clark's ailing troops went from one disaster to another and, by February, he'd been sacked. Joe Royle was approached and, this time, accepted. Royle brought back Ian Bishop from West Ham, signed Jamie Pollock from Bolton and also signed future fans' hero Shaun Goater from Bristol City.

Francis Lee ended his tenure as chairman and David Bernstein took over but, despite all the changes and the fact that there had seemed to have been enough time to save the club from relegation, a 5-2 win at Stoke on the final day was not enough to keep City in Division One. The Blues had been relegated to the third tier of English football for the first time in their history. Kinkladze, clearly never in Royle's plans for the future, was allowed to join Ajax, and cult hero Uwe Rösler returned to Germany.

City were entering unchartered territory...

Above: Despair and dismay for (left to right) Uwe Rösler, Kit Symons, Ian Brightwell and skipper Keith Curle in the tunnel after the final day 2-2 draw with Liverpool relegated City from the Premier League.

Top: Geoff Lomax (2) heads the ball clear as City clinched promotion back to the First Division with a 5–1 win against Charlton Athletic at Maine Road on 11 May 1985

Left: Legendary City goalkeeper Joe Corrigan made his debut against Blackpool in October 1967 and ended his career against Swansea City in March 1983.

Above: Youth team graduate David White was one of several promising talents to emerge from the FA Youth Cup-winning side towards the end of the 1980s.

REACHING THE QUARTER-FINALS OF BOTH THE FA CUP AND LEAGUE CUP SUGGESTED BETTER TIMES LAY AHEAD FOR CITY'S YOUNG TEAM.

Above: Boyhood City fan Paul Lake lived the dream as he progressed through the ranks to the first team. Often described as a "Rolls Royce" of a footballer, Lake was tipped to one day captain England, but a series of horrific knee injuries ruined a promising career.

Above: City defender Kenny Clements, during his second spell with the Club, gets the better of Oxford United's striker John Aldridge and clears the ball.

Above right: Injury-plagued Paul Lake featured in parts of six seasons for City, but played only 134 times, the last against Middlesbrough in August 1992.

Right: Prolific forward Dennis Tueart in his second stay with the Club. He enjoyed time with the New York Cosmos between two lengthy spells with the Blues.

Top: Manager John Bond welcomes record signing Trevor Francis after his £1.2 million transfer from Nottingham Forest in September 1981.

Above: Hat-trick heroes Tony Adcock, Paul Stewart and David White pose after they all scored three times in the 10–1 win over Huddersfield Town in November 1987.

Above: Andy Hinchcliffe
(middle) celebrates with Ian
Brightwell, Paul Lake and Ian
Bishop after scoring City's fifth
goal in the 5-1 rout of United
at Maine Road in 1989.

Left: Howard Kendall's stay as manager of City lasted a year before he quit his post and returned to former club Everton.

Below: The Blues' capture of striker Niall Quinn from Arsenal in March 1990 proved shrewd business as he scored almost a goal every three matches in seven seasons for City

Left: Keith Curle poses for a picture with his new City shirt.

Above: Veteran midfielder Peter Reid joined City on a free transfer in 1990 during Howard Kendall's reign. Initially signed as player-coach, Reid would go on to manage the Blues when Kendall resigned

Top right: New manager Brian Horton (right) and long-serving former player, manager and coach Tony Book.

Right: Crowd favourite Peter Beagrie celebrated his goals with acrobatic back-flip, but City fans were treated to the sight on only five occasions in his 65 games for the Club.

Top left: The pain of relegation in May 1996 proves too much for one City fan.

Left: News filters through that the draw against Liverpool was not enough to save City from relegation.

Above top: Tears for Georgi Kinkladze as the Blues lose their top-flight status against Liverpool.

Above: Chairman Francis Lee finds relegation a bitter pill to swallow. It got even worse two years later.

Above: Georgi Kinkladze applauds the thousands of travelling City fans at the Britannia Stadium as the Blues are relegated to the third tier for the first time in Club history. Despite a 5–2 win over Stoke, other results went against City on the final day of the 1997/98 campaign. It was Kinkladze's last game before joining Ajsx.

Right and far right: More misery for the loyal City fans who were soon defiantly singing "Are you watching Macclesfield?"

JOE CORRIGAN

Joe Corrigan's story was one of triumph over adversity. Joe could easily have melted away from the professional scene and never made the grade in top-flight football had he not had the guts and determination to want to prove the doubters wrong.

Signed as youth player in 1966, Joe worked his way up to be third-choice keeper behind Ken Mulhearn and Harry Dowd during the late 1960s but, apart from two League Cup ties in 1967, was given his league chance near the end of the 1968/69 season when he made four starts. He became first choice the season after, but after a number of high-profile errors, his confidence suffered and his weight steadily increased as the fans began to lose patience with him.

Against West Ham at Maine Road in March 1970, Corrigan punted the ball up-field and then turned to walk back to the six-yard box. As he did, the ball flew over his shoulder and into the net after being kicked back on the volley by West Ham's Ronnie Boyce, momentarily confusing the giant keeper before he realized what had happened. The youngster's confidence and reputation was further damaged, though Joe never turned his back on a kick-out again.

He clawed on to his place for the next 4 seasons, never making less than 30 starts in the league, before the Blues snapped up Motherwell's Keith MacRae to challenge for the No. 1 jersey for a record goalkeeper fee. For the next two years, Joe was playing second fiddle to MacRae but, after the Scot was injured during a 1-0 defeat at Leicester, Corrigan was reinstated and, having worked tirelessly in training to get his reflexes sharper and weight under control, he was slimmer and fitter than ever before.

The steely determination shone through in his performances too. Joe was determined there was no way he would lose his place again and missed just one league game in five seasons 1975–80.

For many, during the 1970s, Joe Corrigan *was* Manchester City. He was respected everywhere he went and was unbelievably consistent, never letting the club down and always prepared to get hurt if it meant keeping the ball out of his net.

He struck up a wonderful relationship with the City fans, who were full of respect and admiration for the way he'd turned his career around.

Despite his club form, Joe was the third-choice England keeper, with a succession of national bosses preferring Peter Shilton and Ray Clemence – both excellent keepers in their own right – but had he played at almost any other period since, he would have been England's No. 1 for perhaps a decade. As it was, his England B caps outnumbered his full caps by one (he played 10 times for the unflatteringly named "B" team) and he was even chosen as an over-age player for the Under-21s in 1978, winning 3 caps.

His 602nd and final match for City was a 4-1 defeat to Swansea at Vetch Field in March 1983. It was a disappointing note on which to leave the Blues as he headed to America for pastures new.

In his sizeable absence, City were relegated from the top division for the first time in 17 years just three months later. As it turned out, things didn't work out in the USA, with Seattle running out of money shortly after his arrival. Despite staying on for a short while as he tried to make his "American Dream" work, Joe returned to England with Brighton and Hove Albion, who were now in the same division as City. Joe returned "home" with the Seagulls in November 1983 to one of the most incredible receptions since Colin Bell's return from injury on Boxing Day 1977, with the applause sustained for several minutes as the Blues' loyal following finally got the chance to say thanks to the big man.

CORRIGAN, JOE
1967–1983
APPEARANCES
602
GOALS
0
POSITION
Goalkeeper
BORN
Manchester

Right: City goalkeeper Joe Corrigan, who followed a long line of legendary keepers the Club has had over the years.

DENNIS TUEART

Signed by City boss Ron Saunders in March 1974, Dennis Tueart became the Club's record signing at a cost of £275,000 from Sunderland. Two days later, he was making his debut in a 0–0 draw with Manchester United. Tueart soon settled into the side and it wasn't long before his busy, all-action and skillful wing play ensured he became a big crowd favourite.

Tueart made 42 appearances in his first full season at Maine Road, but it would be during the 1975/76 campaign that the fiery forward etched his name into the club folklore.

City had reached the League Cup final where Tueart's boyhood favourites, Newcastle United, awaited, and it would be his spectacular overhead kick that won the game 2–1. He finished the season with 24 goals from just 47 appearances and only narrowly lost the MCFC Player of the Year award to the outstanding Joe Corrigan.

City challenged strongly for the 1976/77 Division One title and Tueart was the player who spearheaded the assault. He would finish with 18 goals from 45 starts as City agonizingly finished a point behind eventual champions Liverpool.

City were again among the frontrunners in 1977/78 and Tueart was on fire, scoring three hat-tricks before New Year. But he was unsettled and, despite scoring 15 goals in 25 games, he was ambitious and keen to broaden his horizons. He left for New York Cosmos in March 1978. City's title attempt faltered badly after his departure, the team winning just five of the last 16 games to finish fourth.

Tueart became a hero to the vast crowds that crammed into the Meadowlands Stadium in the Big Apple. A Tueart goal would be welcomed by an electronic scoreboard message of "Sweet Feet" or "Do it, Tueart!"

TUEART, DENNIS
1974–78 and 1980–83
APPEARANCES
269
GOALS
107
POSITION
Forward
BORN
Newcastle

Playing alongside some of the world's best players and living a life of luxury – complete with Cadillac – he enjoyed almost two years in the USA before the bubble burst in the North American Soccer League and he rejoined City for £150,000.

Back in his adopted home of Manchester, and though beset by injury over the next three seasons, he scored 22 goals in 66 starts.

He left the Blues in 1983 as part of a wage-trimming exercise as the club faced up to life in Division Two. He later became a successful businessman and an influential City director in 1997, where he remained for several years.

Left: Dennis Tueart – a born winner with a tenacious streak to match his trickery and eye for a spectacular goal.

Above: Tueart spent two seasons playing the North American Soccer League before returning to City for a second spell in February 1980.

UWE RÖSLER

When he arrived on trial at City, it's fair to say the odds were stacked against Uwe Rösler making a name for himself in English football. The East German-born centre-forward could hardly speak a word of English and was virtually unknown outside the recently reunified Germany. But Rösler was made of stern stuff and he would go on to become one of the City's most popular players of the modern era. He made his debut in a 1-1 draw at QPR and, within the next four games, Paul Walsh and Peter Beagrie also signed to give an ailing City side a much needed boost, and the 10 goals shared between them in the final eight games secured the Blues' top-flight status for at least another year.

Rösler, who had initially joined on loan, was signed on a permanent deal for £500,000, and the following season, he formed part of a terrific forward line that included Beagrie, Walsh, Niall Quinn and Nicky Summerbee. Indeed, Rösler's form meant the previously automatic choice, Quinn, had to make do with the bench on a number of occasions. Manager Brian Horton had an embarrassment of riches up front and the football was open and entertaining, and Rösler feasted off two of the best crossers in the game in the form of Beagrie and Summerbee.

Injury kept him out for several games but he enjoyed a terrific second half of the season, scoring four goals in one game against Notts County and ending the campaign with 22 goals and having forged a fantastic player-fan relationship.

But when Horton was sacked and replaced by Alan Ball, things began to turn sour for Rösler. Although he played all but one of the matches in first half of the 1995/96 season, he was dropped towards the end of the campaign in favour of Nigel Clough and new signing Mikhail Kavlashvilli – a move that enraged the passionate striker and, when he clambered off the bench to score a wonderful equalizing goal against Manchester United at Maine Road, instead of celebrating an obviously joyous moment, he pushed his team-mates away as he ran toward Alan Ball, gesturing to the name on the back of his shirt.

Rösler was reinstated for the last three games, scoring the winner against Sheffield Wednesday and converting a penalty against Liverpool on the final day of the season – but it wasn't enough, and the Blues were relegated.

Ball was sacked after just two matches of the 1996/97 campaign, but Rösler went on to play in all but three of the games during that season, scoring 16 goals and forging a wonderful understanding with Georgian midfielder Gio Kinkladze. The goals dried up the following season, just seven in 33 matches, as City suffered a second relegation in three years,. Rösler made his final appearance for the club coming on as a substitute at Middlesbrough.

Having scored 65 goals in 180 games for the Blues, he returned to Germany to play for Kaiserslautern in the Bundesliga.

He later moved to Norway and played for Lillestrøm, but developed chest cancer a couple of years later, beating the illness by showing the kind of fight and passion he had done while wearing the sky-blue of Manchester City. As he lay in hospital in Norway, a friend held the phone for him to listen to the City fans singing his name at an Etihad home game. He said at the time he was poorly that the singing and the hundreds of get-well messages and cards he received from City fans gave him the strength to pull through.

RÖSLER, UWE
1994–98

APPEARANCES
180

GOALS
65

POSITION
Centre-forward

BORN
Altenburg, East Germany

Right: Cult hero Uwe Rösler was, a bargain signing from FC Nürnberg in March 1993. He led the front line with passion and desire for four seasons.

1998–2008: KEEGAN, SVEN AND GOODBYE MAINE ROAD

5

5. 1998–2008: KEEGAN, SVEN AND GOODBYE MAINE ROAD

It was too soon to say City were back, but the green shoots of recovery had begun, and the momentum carried over from the play-off final continued into the 1999/2000 season. Republic of Ireland winger Mark Kennedy was the major summer arrival and, despite an opening day loss to Wolves and 0-0 draw at Fulham, the Blues won the next five games in succession and would remain among the First Division promotion challengers all season. Shaun Goater was scoring plenty of goals, Ian Bishop and Kevin Horlock were solid in midfield and young goalkeeper Nicky Weaver outstanding. Just 12 months after a dramatic final day against Gillingham, City's season again hinged on a victory in the final game of the season away to Blackburn.

It was another "only Manchester City" type afternoon as more than 15,000 travelling Blues took over Ewood Park and the surrounding hillsides. With Ipswich awaiting any slip-up to take the second automatic spot, City trailed 1-0 at the break and were lucky it wasn't more as the home side struck the woodwork several times. The second half, however, belonged to Royle's men and, after Goater collected his 29th of the campaign to level scores, a Christian Dailly own goal, plus efforts from Kennedy and Paul Dickov added three more to send City back to the Premier League and complete back-to-back promotions. It was just 18 months before that City had lost 2-1 at York and slipped to the lowest league position in Club history, and now the Blues were a top-flight side again. To say it had been a rollercoaster journey would be a huge understatement and the outpouring of joy on the Ewood Park pitch, which was filled with thousands of celebrating City fans, was quite a sight.

Joe Royle had the keys to the city, yet within another drama-filled 12 months, his reign would be over.

The return to the Premier League proved to be a disappointing one, despite the signings of Alfie Haaland, Paulo Wanchope and former FIFA World Player of the Year George Weah. The 4-0 opening-day defeat at Charlton set the tone for the season ahead. Wanchope grabbed a hat-trick on his home debut against Sunderland but, in truth, it was one of only a few highlights, with Weah soon on his travels again midway through the campaign as Royle turned to the trusted partnership of Goater and Dickov one more. Goals and victories were hard to come by and City looked like a side who had come up a season or two too soon, and despite a late flurry of points, Ipswich Town sent the Blues back down again in the penultimate match of the campaign. Lessons hadn't been learned on the pitch and, though Royle was understandably still in credit with the City fans, chairman David Bernstein took a brave decision to sack the still-popular boss shortly after the season ended. Royle had worked wonders with the City side but had perhaps taken them as far as he could.

Within a couple of days, the Blues announced that former Liverpool legend and Newcastle manager Kevin Keegan was the new manager of Manchester City. It was an amazing coup by the City board and one that was well received by the fans. Here was a man who had done it all and was respected throughout the world as one of England's best ever players. The gloom of relegation was replaced by expectancy and optimism, and the 2001/02 campaign began with new signings Eyal Berkovic and former England skipper Stuart Pearce in the team for the opening fixture, a Saturday evening home match with Watford that fairly crackled with electricity and expectation. Some

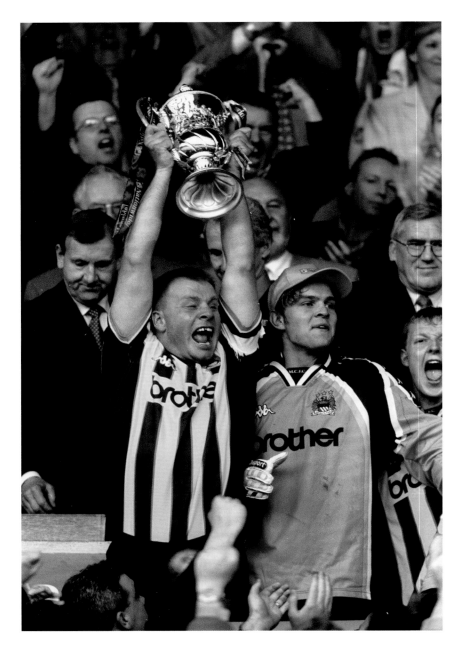

Above: A jubilant City captain Andy Morrison lifts the Division Two play-off trophy after a penalty shoot-out win over Gillingham at Wembley in May 1999.

Above right: City manager Joe Royle celebrates City's 1998/99 promotion at Wembley after the heart-stopping comeback against Gillingham.

called it the "KK factor" – whatever it was, Maine Road was alive again and the manner in which City dispatched Watford 3-0 suggested happy days were ahead. Indeed, they were.

Keegan's attacking philosophy certainly saw City ship a few goals, but more often than not, the Blues scored more than they conceded. The arrival of Algerian maestro Ali Benarbia on a free transfer proved to be the coup de grâce for City and gave the Blues, with Berkovic, a creative midfield supply that many Premier League sides could not match, let alone other Division One sides. Goater and Wanchope linked well in attack and were feasting on goals, and there were several breath-taking performances, notably a

4-2 win at Burnley and particularly the 6-2 victory away to Sheffield Wednesday. With Pearce as captain, the midfielders unplayable and the strikers banging in the goals, the Blues coasted to the Division One championship with club records falling along the way as some 108 goals were scored during one of the most enjoyable seasons many City fans could remember.

The Blues were about to start their sixth season in a row in a different division – could Keegan ensure that sequence would finally end?

Keegan made it clear he wasn't interested in plodding along as a Premier League also-ran and demanded the board back him in the transfer market. He wasted no time adding players who had already proved themselves at the top, with Nicolas Anelka, Sylvain Distin, Robbie Fowler, Marc-Vivien Foé and Peter Schmeichel all joining over the summer. This would also be City's final season at their home of 80 years, Maine Road. The Moss Side base was outdated, and development would have been difficult and expensive. Previous chairman Francis Lee had brokered a deal for City to move into the 2002 Commonwealth Games stadium in East Manchester once the event had finished. Work would go on throughout the 2002/03 campaign and would increase the capacity at home games from 34,000 to 47,000, providing much-needed additional revenue.

Keegan had to ensure City didn't kick off new life at Eastlands as a second-tier club, but as it turned out, there was never a threat that the Blues would be relegated – at least after the first

10 games had been played! City started shakily, winning two and losing six to post just eight points from a possible 30, but three consecutive wins followed and the pressure eased thereafter. The third of those victories was huge – the final Maine Road Manchester derby.

The Blues and Reds would never meet again at Maine Road and City needed to give a performance that matched the occasion – and they did.

Anelka put City ahead before United drew level just three minutes later through Ole Gunnar Solskjaer. In the 26th minute, Gary Neville attempted to shepherd the ball out of play and was pickpocketed by Shaun Goater, who then drilled a low shot home from a narrow angle. Six minutes after the break, Goater struck again and City ended 3-1 winners.

The Blues held their own and there would be highs and lows in the games that remained: a few heavy defeats and a few notable wins, particularly the 2-1 success at Liverpool – the first Anfield victory for 22 years.

The penultimate home game against Sunderland saw Marc-Vivien Foé complete the scoring in a 3-0 win – though nobody knew, it was the last goal scored at Maine Road by a City player and, given the events of a few months later, a fitting tribute for Foé, who would tragically die of a heart attack just two months later.

In typical City fashion, the Blues lost their final home game – 1-0 at the hands of Southampton – but finished a highly creditable ninth and, although the Saints win leapfrogged them into eighth and automatic UEFA Cup qualification, City would be awarded a place in the UEFA Cup by virtue of the Fair Play League standings.

The Blues were back in Europe for the first time in 24 years and the upward trajectory under Keegan continued.

The first game at City's new home was a showpiece friendly against Barcelona, watched by

36,000 fans – the maximum allowed while the third tier's safety certificate was signed off.

The Blues won 2-1, and a few days later, Trevor Sinclair scored the first official goal at the City of Manchester Stadium. The boyhood City fan scored after 14 minutes as the Blues beat Welsh minnows Total Network Solutions (TNS) 5-0 in the first leg of a UEFA Cup Qualifying Round. Shaun Wright-Phillips, Jihai Sun, David Sommeil and Nicolas Anelka were also on target. A few days later, David Sommeil scored City's first Premier League goal at the City of Manchester Stadium as he headed home a 90th-minute equalizer against Portsmouth to secure a 1-1 draw. The milestones were being posted thick and fast.

Above: Paul Dickov scores City's fourth of the afternoon in the 4-1 win at Blackburn as City seal back-to-back promotion in May 2000.

But the first season in their new home would not be easy. City went a worrying 14 games without a win from November to mid-February and, for a while, it seemed as though the Blues would mark the first campaign in East Manchester with relegation. Even after thrashing Manchester United 4-1 in the first Eastlands derby, seven winless games followed.

A crucial 1-0 win over Newcastle three games from the end of the season, however, proved decisive and all but assured Premier League survival.

Worryingly, the so-called Keegan Factor seemed to have run its course, with the manager finding it difficult to motivate his team the way he had when he had first arrived, and two-thirds of the way through another patch campaign, Keegan quit his post, leaving assistant manager Stuart Pearce to take the reins.

After narrowly losing his first game in charge, City then won four and drew three of the next seven games to go into the final game of the season knowing a win over Middlesbrough would secure European football again. The game was locked at 1-1 when the Blues were awarded a stoppage time penalty – which Robbie Fowler missed, meaning Boro took the final UEFA Cup spot. Pearce had done enough to impress chairman John Wardle, however, and was awarded the job on a permanent basis.

To say the next few seasons were fairly uneventful would be an understatement. Dull even, when you consider City's colourful past. A mixture of having a very tight budget and a defensive-minded manager would combine to create the one thing City cannot abide – mediocrity.

Things had started so well under Stuart Pearce that it would have been grossly unfair not to have given him the job after Keegan quit, and the first five games of the 2005/06 season reaffirmed that general consensus. City won three and drew two, meaning that Pearce's first 14 games in charge had brought seven wins, six draws and just one defeat. Impressive stuff. But once the "new manager bump" subsided, the Blues started to struggle. The next 16 matches brought just five wins until a 3-1 win over United raised spirits in an improved run of four wins in seven matches.

But signs of frustration were starting to show, with 2-0 FA Cup quarter-final loss at Blackburn seeing the first real dissent among City fans.

Pearce was a shade lucky that his team had hit the 40-point mark – the so-called safety mark to stay in the Premier League with a 2-1 win over Sunderland. The Blues had played 28 games and had already done just enough, but an awful end to the campaign saw City lose nine of the last 10 matches to finish in 15th, some nine points ahead of third-from-bottom Birmingham, managing just five goals in that period.

It was a portend of things to come.

The first half of the 2006/07 campaign suggested Pearce had plenty of defensive nous but was poor offensively. Indeed, the first eight games at the City of Manchester Stadium saw City concede just one goal and score seven.

However, a 2-1 home win against Everton on New Year's Day would be the last Premier League goals City would score at home that season. The Blues went nine matches without a home League goal to end the campaign with just 10 for the season. Including 43 minutes at the start of the

Top left: Algerian maestro Ali Benarbia who joined City on a free transfer from Paris Saint-Germain in 2001 and helped the Blues to win promotion a year later.

Above left: Eyal Berkovic, the Israeli international (left), celebrates with Frenchman Laurent Charvet as City get the 2001/02 season off to a flyer.

Above: Kevin Keegan with the trophy after City had won the 2001/02 Division One title and Premier League promotion at the end of his first season as team boss.

Left: Former England boss Sven Goran Eriksson takes charge of City for the 2007/08 season.

Right: New home – once the 2002 Commonwealth Games were over, the stadium was turned into a 48,000-capacity football venue with City moving in for the 2003/04 campaign.

next season City would go 781 minutes – 13 hours – between home League goals, though there were five in two January FA Cup ties. City finished 14th but the fans had seen enough. Pearce had to go – and he was duly sacked after the season ended.

Rumblings of a takeover had continued since Christmas and, in June 2007, Chairman John Wardle sold the Club to former Thai Prime Minister Thaksin Shinawatra for £81.6 million and the new owner's first decision was to hire former England boss Sven-Göran Eriksson as his new manager. The Swede was handed a healthy transfer budget and he brought in reasonably-priced stars from around Europe, including Martin Petrov, Elano, Valeri Bojinov, Vedran Ćorluka, Geovanni, Javier Garrido and Rolando Bianchi.

It was exactly what the supporters had hoped for after a steady but largely miserable time under Pearce. It felt like a new era for Manchester City and the opening-day win away to West Ham United confirmed as much, as City played adventurously and with a free spirit to win 2-0.

Michael Johnson ended the long wait for a home goal in the next game against Derby County as City recorded a 1-0 win, and Geovanni's spectacular drive in the third game was enough to beat Manchester United at the City of Manchester and send the Blues top of the Premier league with just three games played.

It was a dream start for Sven, the new owner and the new players and, by Christmas, City fans

were dreaming of Champions League football – or better. The Blues had won 11, drawn six and lost just four of the Premier League 21 matches played. The home form under Sven had been imperious too, winning the first nine on the bounce, but it wouldn't last. In fact, after those first nine home matches had produce with a 100-per cent win rate, the final 10 yielded just two victories!

There had been plenty of highs, with the 2-0 win away to Manchester United ending a 34-year wait for City to win at Old Trafford, but the champagne began to go flat as the season progressed.

In April 2008, City won the FA Youth Cup for the second time with a 3-1 second-leg victory over Chelsea at the Etihad Stadium. After drawing the first leg 1-1 at Stamford Bridge, the City youngsters won at home to complete a 4-2 aggregate win – and they were watched by more than 20,000 fans.

In the Premier League, however, things weren't going so well as City won only four of the final 18 games but had still been in contention for a European berth going into the final game away to Middlesbrough, but with rumours rife that Sven had already been told he would be sacked at the end of the season, City slumped to a final-day thrashing at the Riverside Stadium, losing 8-1 to Boro. It was a sad end to what, at times, had been a hugely enjoyable season.

It was the end of Sven, and there was more drama to come in the months that followed.

Left: City keeper Nick Weaver sets off on a celebratory run after the Blues triumph on penalties against Gillingham in the Dvision Two Playoff final at Wembley in 1999.

Right: Paul Dickov's fires the last-gasp injury time equalizer to save City's season and force extra time against Gillingham at Wembley in 1999.

Below: The players pay homage to the 40,000 City fans who made the long journey south for the 1999 Divison Two Play-off final.

Left: Inspirational captain Andy Morrison on the ball during the 1998/99 campaign, City's first-ever in the third tier of English football.

Below: Shaun Goater celebrates another goal for City. The Bermudian striker was a prolific goalscorer during his five seasons with the Club.

Left: Mark Kennedy celebrates with manager Joe Royle after putting City 3-1 up at Blackburn Rovers in 2000.

Above: An estimated 20,000 City fans packed into Ewood Park to celebrate promotion back to the top-flight after a four-year absence,

IT WAS ANOTHER "ONLY MANCHESTER CITY"
TYPE AFTERNOON AS MORE THAN 15,000
TRAVELLING BLUES TOOK OVER EWOOD PARK
AND THE SURROUNDING HILLSIDES.

Top far left: City leave the Portman Road pitch after Ipswich Town relegate the Blues who had spent just one season back in the Premier League.

Bottom far left: Stuart Pearce takes over the reins as manager after Kevin Keegan had resigned the post in 2005.

Top near left: Kevin Keegan celebrates another City goal during the prolific 2001/02 campaign.

Bottom near left: Nicolas Anelka – City's record signing – on target against Charlton Athletic as the Blues start the 2003/04 season with a 3-0 win at The Valley.

Right: David James has swappeds his goalkeeper's jersey for an outfield shirt after a bizarre substitution by Stuart Pearce in the last game of the 2005/06 season. It almost works, too, as City win a late penalty which is missed by Robbie Fowler and as a result, the 1-1 draw means Middlesbrough snatch the last UEFA Cup spot.

Above top: David Sommeil's 90th-minute goal earns a 1-1 draw with Portsmouth in the first Premier League game at City's new home in August 2003. Trevor Sinclair, left, and Paulo Wanchope, right, run to celebrate with him

Above: New manager Sven-Goran Eriksson parades four new international signings before the 2007/08 season (L-R): Javier Garrido (from Spain), Valeri Bojinov (Bulgaria), Elano (Brazil) and Vedran Ćorluka (Croatia).

Above top: Brazilian free transfer midfielder Geovanni Mauricio lets fly with a vicious shot as City take on Manchester United in August 2007

Above: Geovanni wheels away in celebration as his goal against United ensures Sven-Goran Eriksson starts with three wins from three in 2007/08.

SHAUN GOATER

Shaun Goater – or "the Goat" as he became affectionately known at Maine Road – is something of a Manchester City phenomenon. During five years with the Blues, he literally went from zero to hero, becoming a Club legend in the process.

After being rejected as a youngster by Manchester United, Goater had to do things the hard way. Born on the beautiful island of Bermuda, Goater had to learn his trade under the leaden skies of Rotherham, a million miles from the aqua-blue ocean and white sandy beaches of his home.

Despite the constant damp and lack of sun in South Yorkshire, Goater learned his trade with the Millers, developing a reputation as a lower-league goal-poacher over the next seven years.

He would have been forgiven for thinking that was as good as it got in England, until Bristol City began scouring for a talented goal-scorer and identified the Bermudian – who had scored 86 goals in 262 appearances – as their main target.

He cost the Robins £175,000 and quickly settled in at Ashton Gate, where the goals came easily and he won a place in the 1997/98 PFA Team of the Year after bagging 45 goals in 81 games in two seasons for Bristol City. It was that form that caught the attention of City boss Joe Royle, who snapped up Goater for a bargain £400,000. It would be a while before fans realized that, for the first time in many, many years, the Blues had a natural goal-scorer who, given the opportunities, could bang in 20 to 30 goals each season. Goater arrived too late to save the Blues from second-tier demotion, but it was his goals that steered City out of Division Two in 1999, and his tally of 29 in the following campaign ensured a second successive promotion for the Blues. Injury beset the Bermudian international during the doomed 2000/01 Premiership campaign, but he still finished the season in red-hot form with

seven in his last nine games. Back in Division One, he captained the side for the first time at Grimsby Town – a deserved honour for the man City fans adored – and, once again, he ended up top scorer for the fourth consecutive term with 32 goals – the most any City striker had scored since Francis Lee in the early 1970s. His anthem, "Feed the Goat and he will score", was a firm favourite at Maine Road, and perhaps his greatest moment in sky-blue came in the last ever Maine Road Manchester derby when he pickpocketed United captain Gary Neville for his first goal and then added a second after the break – his 100th for the Club – in a 3-1 win for the Blues.

Though he would score in the return to Manchester at Old Trafford – just nine seconds after coming on as a sub – his opportunities became limited at City and he decided to move on and play football elsewhere for a few years. He joined Reading and played for Southend United before retiring in 2006, leaving quite a legacy behind him at City.

GOATER, SHAUN
1998–2003
APPEARANCES
212
GOALS
103
POSITION
Striker
BORN
Bermuda

Below: Shaun Goater (far left) became a cult hero for City fans during his time with the Club, averaging a goal almost every other game in five seasons.

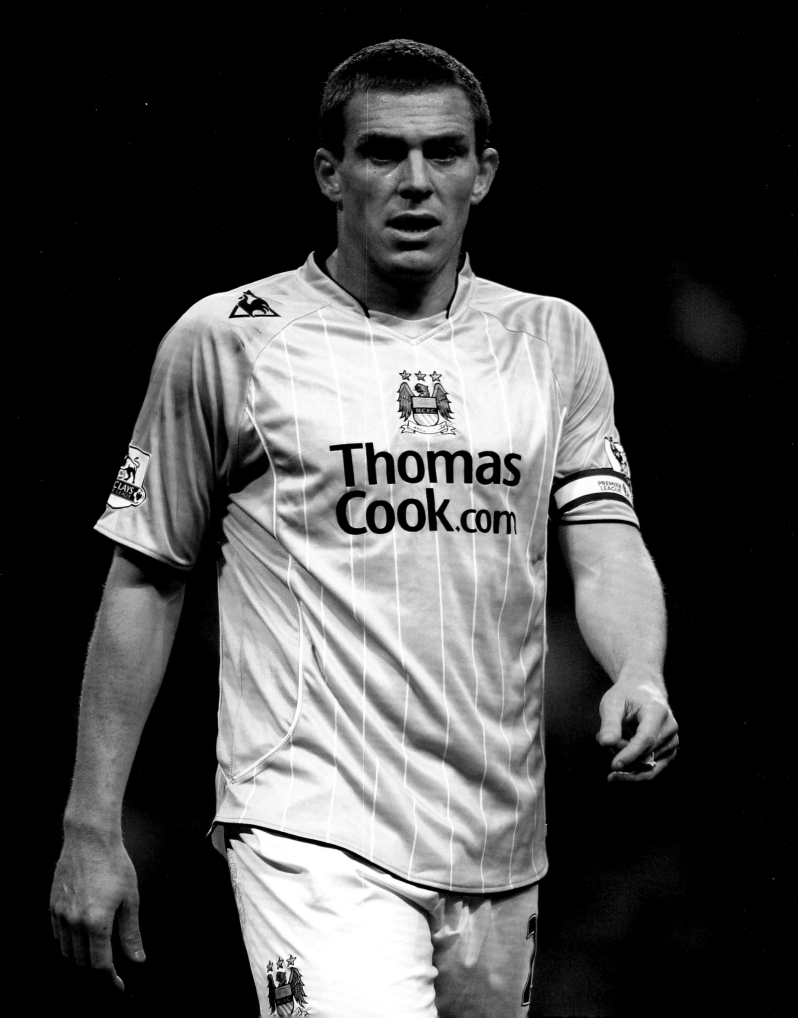

RICHARD DUNNE

Richard Dunne joined City in October 2000 when Joe Royle signed the centre-half from Everton for £3.5 million. Dunne's capture was good business by Royle, even if his arrival didn't cause too much excitement. The Republic of Ireland international was regarded as a "Steady Eddie" more than anything else, and in his first full season, City were relegated. With Royle sacked and replaced by Kevin Keegan, many wondered if Dunne's career with City was over before it had started, but Keegan played him regularly in an enjoyable 2001/02 promotion campaign, with Dunne making 49 appearances.

Back in the Premier League, Dunne's third campaign with City was a difficult one. Disciplined for off-field issues, Dunne was suspended by the club and his Manchester City future looked bleak. He was, in reality, at a crossroads in his career and had the choice either of buckling down and focusing on getting back on track or risking blowing his chance with City and maybe football altogether.

Dunne chose to almost reinvent himself. An intensive fitness programme saw him return for the 2003/04 campign determined to take the second chance Keegan had given him. Slimmer and fitter, Dunne soon became the rock of City's defence and almost indispensable.

An intelligent defender, Dunne was deceptively fast, but also excellent with the ball at his feet, with a super range of passing. By the 2004/05 season, Dunne's transformation was complete and his consistency saw him receive the ultimate fan accolade – the Manchester City Player of the Year award – but there was much more to come from the quietly-spoken Irishman.

Dunne kicked on again in 2005/06. His partnership with Sylvain Distin was formidable and, although the Blues weren't challenging for any silverware, the central-defensive partnership between the Irishman and Frenchman was arguably one of the main reasons City remained in the top flight and Dunne again won the Player of the Year vote.

During the summer of 2006, Dunne was given the captain's armband. A model of consistency, he had become a major fan favourite and first name on the team sheet during what was still a lean time for the club. Incredibly, he was voted Player of the Year for the third season in a row at the end that campaign, despite gathering more red cards than he perhaps wanted to along the way and having an unfortunate knack for scoring own goals, but the reason was that Dunne was always there for his team, putting his body on the line and never giving less than his all.

The 2007/08 season saw Sven-Göran Eriksson take over from Stuart Pearce as team manager, but Dunne's place was never under threat. By the end of another excellent campaign, he was voted Player of the Year for a fourth successive time – an achievement never previously managed by a Manchester City player.

He penned a new four-year deal with the Blues, but the 2008/09 season would be his ninth and final year with the Club. He played 47 times under manager Mark Hughes, but the arrival of Kolo Touré and Joleon Lescott signalled the end of his time with the Blues and he instead joined Aston Villa for a bargain fee of £5 million.

Dunne was the glue that held City's defence together for nearly a decade and is a shining example of what effort and application can achieve in football.

DUNNE, RICHARD
2000–09
APPEARANCES
352
GOALS
7
POSITION
Central defender
BORN
Dublin, Republic of Ireland

Left: Republic of Ireland international defender Richard Dunne spent almost a decade with City winning the Club's Player of the Year four times in succession and being an inspirational figure for the team.

SHAUN WRIGHT-PHILLIPS

Shaun Wright-Phillips was very much, as the terrace song goes, "one of our own" and "Wrighty" – as he was known to one and all – was a huge crowd favourite during two spells with the Blues spanning more than a decade.

Sandwiched between those spells was a stint with Chelsea, where he won four trophies in three seasons under José Mourinho. However, when the chance arose to re-join the Blues – the Manchester Blues, that is – he didn't need to think twice about representing the club where he'd achieved so much.

Wright-Phillips is the adopted son of former England international Ian Wright and brother of another City star Bradley. He was the first graduate of the Academy formed in 1998 and became the standard bearer for all the youngsters hoping to rise through the ranks at Platt Lane. In 2004, when he won his first England cap, he pinned another flag in the ground for the Academy.

Nottingham Forest had allowed the skilful winger to leave the club because they felt he was too small, but City could see his potential. A superb dribbler, he was quick and had an eye for goals, with his all-round energy and infectious enthusiasm combining to create an exciting player who quickly had the fans' adulation.

Though Joe Royle gave him his debut, it was Kevin Keegan who reaped the benefits as Wright-Phillips became a first-team regular. With a heart as big as a lion, he thrilled City fans for six seasons, giving his all every time he played, and blossomed into one of English football's most exciting talents between 2003 and 2005 when he scored 22 goals – many of them spectacular individual efforts – in 83 games for the Blues.

There came a point when it was time to move on and, although he left for Chelsea in 2005 for a record £21 million at a time when the club was in desperate need of funds, he did so with a heavy heart and not an ounce of bitterness from the fans who had supported him every step of the way since he'd made his debut as an 18-year-old against Burnley.

Whenever City played Chelsea, Wrighty was afforded a warm reception from City fans, whether home or away, and when new manager Mark Hughes offered him the chance to go back to the Blues in 2008, he couldn't return north quickly enough. He made a superb second debut in a 3-0 win at Sunderland, scoring twice on what proved to be a dream return.

When Hughes was sacked in December 2009, Shaun's opportunities gradually became limited to cameo roles here and there under Roberto Mancini, and during the Italian's second campaign, he played less and less. Then almost three years to the day after returning to City, on the final day of the August 2011 transfer window, QPR put in bid for his services and he was, once again, off to west London. But the receptions he received whenever he returned "home" were never less than rapturous for one of the club's most popular-ever players.

WRIGHT-PHILLIPS, SHAUN
1999–2005 and 2008–11

APPEARANCES
275

GOALS
47

POSITION
Winger

BORN
London

Right: Crowd favourite Shaun Wright-Phillips was the Club's first Academy graduate and a huge fan favourite during his two spells with the Blues.

SHAUN WRIGHT-PHILLIPS WAS THE FIRST GRADUATE OF THE ACADEMY FORMED IN 1998 AND BECAME THE STANDARD BEARER FOR ALL THE YOUNGSTERS HOPING TO RISE THROUGH THE RANKS AT PLATT LANE.

2008-2013: NEW BEGINNINGS

6

6. 2008–2013: NEW BEGINNINGS

Mark Hughes replaced Eriksson and immediately recruited a number of excellent additions to the squad, with Vincent Kompany and Pablo Zabaleta among the new arrivals. Shaun Wright-Phillips was also re-signed from Chelsea for half the fee he had been sold and, with the confirmation that the Abu Dhabi United Group were close to purchasing the club, City signed Robinho from Real Madrid on transfer-deadline day for a Club record fee of £32.5 million as a statement of the Blues' newfound investment. It was an exciting time for City fans.

Previous spread: Vincent Kompany holds aloft the Premier League trophy after City's dramatic defeat of Queen's Park Rangers clinched the 2011/12 championship at the Etihad.

Left: Sergio Agüero wheels away in celebration having scored the goal that won City's first top-flight title for 44 years.

On 1 September 2008, Sheikh Mansour was confirmed as the new owner of Manchester City. Khaldoon Al Mubarak was installed as the club's new chairman and manager Hughes was given substantial funds to oversee the rebuilding of the squad.

The takeover had largely missed the summer transfer window and Hughes' first 18 games in charge were far from impressive as City won just 5 matches, losing 10.

The January window allowed Hughes to bolster the squad with Nigel de Jong, Shay Given and Craig Bellamy, but the results on the pitch perhaps didn't match the ambition off it.

The form in the second part of the campaign was patchy and, although Hughes guided the Blues to the quarterfinals of the Europa League, his team exited both domestic cup competitions at the first hurdle to lower-league opposition.

Three more points would have seen City finish 7th and again qualify for Europe, but instead the final position was 10th and, despite the excitement and potential generated by the new ownership, the season had ended disappointingly.

Hughes needed to make the 2009/10 campaign a successful one and several major signings

were made during the summer of 2009, including Carlos Tevez and Emmanuel Adebayor, both for substantial outlays. Joleon Lescott and Gareth Barry were also signed before the start of the campaign and City now had a squad capable of challenging for Champions League football.

The club had also shown their muscle in the transfer market and were now considered as one of European football's biggest hitters, capable of competing for the signatures of the world's top players.

City fans had to pinch themselves to believe it was all real. For so long, the club had laboured in the shadow of Manchester United but, as the Tevez deal proved, the Blues could now not only match the Reds in the transfer market but also attract one of their best players.

The Blues fairly flew out of the blocks at the start of the season, winning the first four matches and playing entertaining, attacking football. The 4-2 win over Arsenal at the City of Manchester Stadium demonstrated the pace and power that City now had and the Manchester derby that followed was a thrilling contest, only settled by a Michael Owen goal six minutes into added time as United won 4-3.

Although City won the next game against West Ham, an incredible run of seven successive Premier League draws followed. On paper, one loss in 13 league games and 23 points on the board was not terrible, and a 2-1 win over Premier League leaders Chelsea followed by a 3-3 draw at Bolton was again reasonable. However, there were two ways of looking at it – especially after a dismal 3-0 loss away to Spurs. Six wins from the opening 16 matches, eight draws and two losses represented 26 points won, but 22 points dropped.

City's next game, a 4-3 win over Sunderland, would be Hughes' last in charge. It was a difficult decision for City, but the feeling was that a more

experienced manager with a proven track record was needed, and former Inter Milan boss Roberto Mancini was named as the Blues' new choice.

The Italian won his first four games in charge, changing the playing system and tightening up bolts at the back, and seven victories in his first eight, including a 2-1 League Cup semi-final first-leg win over Manchester United at the City of Manchester Stadium. The Reds won the return 3-1, so City's long wait for silverware continued.

With two games remaining, City hosted Tottenham Hotspur knowing two wins would secure Champions League football for the first time since the revised format had been introduced, but a late winner from Peter Crouch meant the north Londoners took the fourth-place berth with the Blues finishing fifth.

It was a blow but the promise of better things to come was evident, with Mancini determined to end City's long wait for a trophy.

Mancini quickly identified the areas he wanted to strengthen and went for several top European players. David Silva joined from Valencia, Yaya Touré arrived from Barcelona, Aleksandar Kolarov signed from Napoli, Mario Balotelli from Inter Milan and James Milner from Aston Villa. Mancini also brought goalkeeper Joe Hart back from a season-long loan deal at Birmingham as City set their stall out for the 2010/11 season.

With the huge outlay the club had made in transfers, Mancini knew he had to deliver. Five wins and two draws from the first eight games and just five goals conceded suggested the Blues were not only not far off winning silverware, but that they would be a Premier League-title dark horses. The team was packed with quality and the arrival of Silva and Yaya Touré took City's play to a new level – even though neither new man would completely bed in straight away.

From keeper Hart to full-backs Micah Richards, Zabaleta and Kolarov, centre-backs Lescott and Kompany, to a midfield with Silva, de Jong, Touré, Barry and Milner and a forward line that had Tevez, Wright-Phillips and the enigmatic Balotelli – this was a City squad built to win, with the perfect blend of flair, industry and steel and a manager who knew how to best utilize the players at his disposal.

A Europa League group-stage game in mid-October would have a profound effect on City fans. Lech Poznań were the visitors at the City of Manchester and the Polish side brought around 4,000 fans with them (including many from the sizeable Mancunian Polish community) and they introduced something that hadn't been witnessed before as they – en masse – turned their backs, linked arms around each other's shoulders and bounced up and down.

On one evening, "The Poznań" had been born and would, in future weeks, months and years become as synonymous with Manchester City as "Blue Moon" as City fans created their own version of the dance.

Despite all the positives, the Blues stuttered in the early part of the season, so much so that there was audible discontent as City were held to a 0-0 draw by Birmingham City at Eastlands.

Six wins from the first 13 games was disappointing, but seven wins and three draws from the next 11 settled the ship and City went into the New Year on level points with leaders Manchester United, but having played two games more. However, an inconsistent run of five wins in 12 when it mattered most ended hopes of the title.

The Blues had progressed to the round of 16 in the Europa League, but trailing 2-0 to Dynamo Kyiv in the first leg, City halved the deficit in the City of Manchester Stadium return just before a petulant foul by Balotelli saw the Italian striker dismissed and the Blues exited 2-1 on aggregate.

But there was still plenty to play for and, when City and United were paired in the FA Cup semi-final, it would be the first meeting of the Manchester clans at Wembley. It would prove an unforgettable occasion, City edging the game, with a 52nd-minute Yaya Touré winner settling the game and sending the Blues to the final for the first time in 30 years.

In what would be an historic week for the club, City achieved two momentous achievements.

First off – an in an amazing twist of irony – City and Tottenham again went head-to-head for a Champions League spot, this time with the Blues in the box-seat. City knew a win would clinch Champions League football for the first time, and it would be Spurs striker Peter Crouch who again scored the only goal of the game – but this time, in his own net – as City exacted sweet revenge for the game 12 months earlier.

Above: New signing Robinho steps out at the City of Manchester Stadium for his debut against Chelsea in September 2008. The Brazilian joined City for a record fee from Real Madrid, just minutes before the summer transfer window deadline closed and offered proof that the Blues could now compete with the biggest clubs in the world for top talent.

Above: New signing Carlos Tevez delivers a message to his former manager after scoring in the League Cup semi-final first leg against Manchester United.

Right: Striker Edin Dzeko, known as "The Bosnian Diamond", in action against Liverpool.

Four days later, the Blues took on Stoke City in the 2011 FA Cup final. Could the wait for a trophy finally end against Tony Pulis's side? The answer was yes. The tension in the stands was drifting down to the pitch as the players perhaps felt the weight of history on their shoulders. Worse still, everything Man City struck was saved by Stoke keeper Thomas Sørensen, whose heroics were frustrating the Blues with a series of magnificent saves.

Yaya Touré, hero in the semi-final, was again the man of the hour as he slammed home a shot in the 74th minute to win the FA Cup for City and end the 35-year wait for silverware.

"That's why we bought him," said Mancini afterwards. "He's a wonderful player."

On an afternoon of emotion for the success-starved Blues, the celebrations lasted long into the night and for several days after.

Victories in the two remaining Premier League matches against Stoke (again!) and Bolton also secured third spot in the table and automatic entry

into the Champions League group stage.

The Poznań, a major trophy and Champions League football. It had been quite a season.

City looked to build on a fine 2010/11 campaign by adding two major new signings for the start of the 2011/12 season. Sergio Agüero arrived from Atletico Madrid for a fee in excess of £35 million and Samir Nasri arrived from Arsenal. For Roberto Mancini, they were the final parts of the puzzle.

Though City gave a two-goal lead away to lose 3-2 in the FA Community Shield, it would be one of very few disappointments in the campaign ahead. Agüero made his debut as a second-half substitute against newly promoted Swansea City at the now rebranded Etihad Stadium. He took just a couple of minutes to find the back of the net and added a 25-yard stunner before the end to announce his arrival in style. The Argentine never looked back.

The thrilling brand of football of football Mancini's side were playing was emphasized just three Premier League games in. Having survived an onslaught to leave White Hart Lane with a 0-0

draw just 12 months earlier, City returned to face Tottenham and, over 90 minutes, dismantled a side who would eventually finish fourth in the table. The 5-1 victory screamed title favourites – never mind contenders.

The very first Champions League game at the Etihad ended 1-1 with Napoli – Aleks Kolarov scoring the Blues' goal – but the next group-stage clash would see a major falling out between Mancini and Carlos Tevez, who appeared to refuse to warm-up as City were beaten 2-0 away to Bayern Munich. Tevez was fined and would effectively go on "gardening leave" for several months, but Mancini felt he had enough firepower with Agüero, Mario Balotelli and Edin Dzeko at his disposal.

And results in the Premier League suggested the Blues weren't missing the former United striker. They made a blistering start of 12 wins and two draws from the opening 14 games. Included in that run was an historic victory at Old Trafford where City turned in an incredible performance to beat United 6-1 and equal the biggest ever Manchester-

derby triumph. For City fans, it was a day never to forget and, in one fell swoop, banished years of hurt and, more importantly, gave the Blues the belief they needed in the title race.

Although City ended their first Champions League group stage on 10 points, it was still not enough to progress to the knockout phase.

Mancini lamented that 10 points would, more often than not, have ensured progress, but Bayern Munich and Napoli finished with 13 and 11, respectively.

Domestically, City and United were going toe-to-toe with each other in the title race. The Blues lost their unbeaten record at Chelsea in December and also lost to an injury-time goal at Sunderland on

Above: Another new arrival, Nigel de Jong, quickly became a huge crowd favourite among the City fans. The Dutch midfield enforcer's non-nonsense approach and full-blooded tackling were a key part of the Blues' successes.

Right: Roberto Mancini became the first City manager to win the FA Cup for 42 years after the Blues beat Stoke in the 2011 final.

New Year's Day, and January also saw hopes of the League and FA Cups end with defeats to Liverpool and United, respectively. It allowed Mancini's side to focus almost exclusively on the Premier League, and things were going to plan until a hiccup at what seemed the worst time.

A 2-0 win over Bolton put City five points clear of the Reds going into the final two months of the season as the pressure cranked up. A surprise 1-0 defeat at Swansea was followed by a narrow – and crucial – 2-1 win over Chelsea. But successive draws against Stoke and Sunderland followed. The latter – a 3-3 draw that City rescued with goals in the 85th and 86th minutes – allowed United to open a five-point lead at the top. Worse was to

follow as City's title challenge apparently ended with a Balotelli red card and late goal conceded in a 1-0 defeat to Arsenal. Six games remained and City were eight points behind United. The Reds needed three more wins to take the title and all seemed lost.

Carlos Tevez had ended his exile and been training with the Blues again after apologizing for the incident earlier in the season, and Mancini included him in the midweek game against West Brom, which would prove a pivotal evening in the title race.

City swept aside West Brom 4-0 at the Etihad as news that United had lost 1-0 to Wigan Athletic filtered through. City then travelled to Norwich and,

inspired by a sensational Tevez display, won 6-1 to keep the pressure on the Reds.

The following weekend saw United play first and City fans watched in disbelief as the Reds threw a 4-2 lead away to draw 4-4. City then beat Wolves 2-0 to reduce the gap to just three points, with a potential title-deciding Manchester derby up next at the Etihad. The Blues knew that victory, thanks to a superior goal difference, would take pole position from Sir Alex Ferguson's men with only a couple of games to go.

United set their stall out for the point they knew would probably end City's hopes, but instead, skipper Vincent Kompany's towering header just before the break proved to be enough to take the three points. The Blues were on the brink.

Whose nerve would hold?

Six points and City were guaranteed the title, but a tricky test away with Newcastle United still had to be negotiated and the St James' Park test proved to be every bit as tense and nervy as predicted, but – just as he had delivered last season in the FA Cup semi and final – Yaya Touré broke the deadlock 70 minutes in with a long-range shot and the Ivorian settled the travelling fans' nerves just before full-time to complete a hard-fought 2-0 win over the Magpies.

Victory over relegation-threatened QPR on the final day would end a 44-year wait for the top-flight title but there would be plenty of twists and turns in what was meant to be a fairly straightforward match.

With history beckoning and a packed Etihad Stadium desperate for their team to deliver, things began well, with City dominating and taking the lead just before the break through Pablo Zabaleta. The second half, however, did not run to the expected script.

QPR, by that stage, needed at least a point to stay up and, within three minutes, a nerve-shredded home crowd were in despair as Joleon Lescott misjudged a header and allowed Djibril Cissé to race away and equalize. QPR then lost former City midfielder Joey Barton in a fracas that involved numerous players from both teams.

But it was a 10-man Rangers who scored the next goal, with Jamie Mackie heading home in the 66th minute to leave the Etihad shell-shocked. City had many days when they'd shot themselves in the foot, but this would usurp all that had gone before.

The clock ticked past 90 minutes with QPR still 2-1 up and United 2-0 up at Sunderland. The title, as things stood with seconds left of the 2011/12 campaign, was headed for Old Trafford.

What followed in the time that remained was the stuff of legend...

Dzeko made it 2-2, heading home David Silva's corner from close range. Was there enough time remaining? Time was almost up when Nigel de Jong brought the ball forward. His short pass found Balotelli, who held the ball up before nudging it to the side, where Agüero collected, skipped past one challenge and then hammered home a low drive with 93 minutes and 20 seconds on the clock.

Cue pandemonium.

The City fans, players and staff went wild. Even the QPR fans celebrated, safe in the knowledge their team was now safe from the drop and the Blues were the champions of England for the first time since 1968. With the Agüero goal, 44 years of hurt had been wiped out in the blink of an eye and it had all been done the Manchester City way – with maximum drama. First the FA Cup, now the Premier League... it was an incredible time to be a City fan.

Above left: The never-say-die and all out effort of Carlos Tevez made him integral to City's team.

Above: For parts of the final day of the 2011/12 season it seemed as if it would be anguish for Blues fans as City looked like they might blow their Premier League title hopes against QPR.

If City were guilty of anything as they prepared to defend their Premier League crown, it was not adding one or two top-quality signings to an already strong squad. Even the best teams need freshening up or fine tuning and the summer signings City made – Javi Garcia, Maicon Sisenando, Scott Sinclair and Matija Nastasić – were all unproven in the top flight and the influential, and popular Nigel de Jong would leave a couple of weeks into the new campaign. Pre-season had seen plenty of goals scored and Roberto Mancini's side had a definite swagger, which carried on as City beat Chelsea 3-2 at Villa Park in the Community Shield.

Three draws and two wins in the first five Premier League games was not a disaster, but it represented six points dropped and, more worryingly, the Blues had struggled at some stage in each game, failing to keep a clean sheet. A pivotal clash that could have given City real impetus early on was also nearly a historic night as City locked horns with José Mourinho's Real Madrid in the first Champions League group-stage match at the Bernabéu. The Blues twice took the lead through Edin Dzeko and Aleksandar Kolarov – the latter scoring with just five minutes to go – to give City a 2-1 lead. A win in Madrid's own backyard would have been a huge statement for a side still getting used to playing on Europe's

biggest stage but, in a naïve finish, Karim Benzema and Cristiano Ronaldo dramatically bagged goals in the time that remained to deal City a crushing 3-2 defeat.

The following month, in the same competition, Joe Hart turned in the performance of his life as City clung on against Borussia Dortmund at the Etihad. The rampant Germans were impossible to contain on the night and Hart made at least four stunning saves before finally being beaten by Marco Reus – Mario Balotelli rescued a draw in the 90th minute with a penalty but Dortmund proved what a tough group the Blues had found themselves in. It also demonstrated that Mancini's side had a long way to go before they could compete with Europe's top sides.

City's hopes of progression to the round of 16 rested on beating Ajax home and away, but just one point from two games against the Dutch side effectively ended the Champions League campaign and the Blues would end the group without a win and bottom. An early League Cup exit aside, hopes of back-to-back titles increased as Dzeko grabbed a dramatic late winner just three minutes from the end of normal time to give City a 2-1 win over Tottenham at the Etihad to preserve the Blues' unbeaten Premier League start and, by the time the December Manchester derby came around, City were still unbeaten in the Premier

League, having extended the run to 21 matches stretching back to the previous April. But United, still smarting from losing the title on the last day of the 2011/12 campaign, had a point to prove and Robin van Persie's goal three minutes into added time gave the Reds a 3-2 win at the Etihad. Another narrow loss at Sunderland on Boxing Day hit City's title hopes, but a run of six successive wins followed, two of them in the FA Cup. However, there was disappointment to follow.

Having failed to see off QPR at Loftus Road to end January, City then dropped more points in a 2-2 home draw with Liverpool – a game that yielded a contender for goal of the season as Agüero somehow equalized from near the corner flag. Then came the season's low point with a demoralizing 3-1 defeat to Southampton, meaning seven points had been dropped in three games, and the Blues' hopes of retaining the title suddenly looked over with a relentless United extending their lead at the top to nine points. March saw City lose further ground in the title race, with Everton perhaps providing the final fatal blow in the form of a 2-0 win at Goodison Park. The Blues hopes of catching the Reds were now only mathematical and the champions went into the Old Trafford derby 15 points adrift of the Reds. If nothing else, City needed to restore local pride and, thanks to goals from Milner and a breath-taking solo effort from Agüero, the Blues triumphed

2-1 to leave the travelling fans wondering about what might have been.

The last hope of silverware was the FA Cup and, thanks to goals from Nasri and Agüero, City's 2-1 win over Chelsea booked a second FA Cup final in three years and pencilled in a date with Wigan Athletic. But an off-colour Blues suffered heartbreak as Ben Watson headed home a 90th-minute winner for Wigan at Wembley. It was also the end of the road for Roberto Mancini, who was dismissed after the game, leaving assistant manager Brian Kidd to oversee the final two matches of the campaign as City looked for a new boss. Kidd's Blues won 2-0 at Reading, but then lost 3-2 to Norwich City at the Etihad.

Above: Edin Dzeko rises to meet the ball during the disappointing FA Cup final defeat against Wigan Athletic. The Bosnian was a prolific scorer for City during his time with the Club.

THEN CAME THE SEASON'S LOW POINT WITH A DEMORALIZING 3-1 DEFEAT TO SOUTHAMPTON MEANING SEVEN POINTS HAD BEEN DROPPED IN THREE GAMES, AND THE BLUES' HOPES OF RETAINING THE TITLE SUDDENLY LOOKED OVER.

Left: Manager Mark Hughes looks calm and relaxed as he poses for a picture in City's boot room.

Bottom: Emmanuel Adebayor infuriates the Arsenal fans after scoring a goal at the opposite end of the City of Manchester Stadium in 2009 and then sprinting 90 yards to celebrate in front of them.

Below: Sergio Agüero tries an overhead kick under pressure from Chelsea's David Luiz at the Etihad Stadium in City's 2011/12 championship season.

Above: City fans start yet another "Poznań" dance during a game at the Etihad. For several years it became the Club's trademark celebration – or it was performed to liven up the atmosphere when needed!.

Right: Carlos Tevez's stay at City was brilliant but occasionally tempestuous.

Far right: Manager Roberto Mancini watches from the sidelines with his famous blue and white scarf.

Left: Nigel de Jong models the new kit for the media at a photoshoot.

Above: Robinho marks his debut against Chelsea with a goal that sends the home fans (and players) delirious.

Left: James Milner whips in a cross during a clash against Liverpool, the club which would later sign him.

Top left: Final day action against QPR – Pablo Zabaleta clears the danger under pressure from Taye Taiwo.

Top right: David Silva tries to weave his magic against Rangers skipper and former Blue Joey Barton with City still trailing 2-1

Above: Substitute Edin Dzeko heads home David Silva's corner to make it 2-2 against QPR in the second minute of added time.

Top: The miracle is completed as Sergio Agüero scores the winning goal against Queen's Park Rangers with 93 minutes and 20 seconds on the clock.

Above left: Manager Roberto Mancini still believes his players can do it and urges his time on after they had levelled the scores in added time.

Above right: Champions! Sergio Agüero (left) and the man who started the move that led to his – and City's – title-winning goal, Nigel de Jong.

THE CITY FANS, PLAYERS AND STAFF WENT
WILD. EVEN THE QPR FANS CELEBRATED, SAFE
IN THE KNOWLEDGE THEIR TEAM WAS NOW
SAFE FROM THE DROP AND THE BLUES WERE
THE CHAMPIONS OF ENGLAND FOR THE FIRST
TIME SINCE 1968.

Above: Manchester City celebrate winning the Premier League championship in May 2012 – the Club's first top-flight title for 44 years.

Top right: Roberto Mancini and assistant coach Attilio Lombardo (in scarf, left) parade the Premier League trophy.

Middle right: James Milner and Gareth Barry soak up the atmosphere on the parade through Manchester's city centre..

Right: More than 100,000 Manchester City fans lined the streets to greet the team on their Championship celebration parade in May 2012.

PABLO ZABALETA

Pablo Zabaleta's arrival at City in 2008 was relatively low-key, with the Blues paying a modest fee for the Argentine right-back. It was an astute signing by manager Mark Hughes, given almost a decade of incredible service that would follow.

Zaba steadily became a firm crowd favourite with the City supporters who quickly resonated with his passion, heart and willingness to put his body on the line time and time again.

With a £6.5 million move from Espanyol completed, Zaba joined City the day before it was announced that Sheikh Mansour was the club's new owner. He made his debut for City in September 2008 – the same day as fellow new arrival Robinho – as Chelsea triumphed 3-1 at Eastlands.

In a series of firsts, he received his first red card against Liverpool a month later and scored his first goal – a cracking effort from the edge of the box – against Wigan Athletic in January 2009. By that point, the tough-tackling right-back had already cemented his place in the fans' hearts and would remain a crowd idol throughout his time in Manchester.

His father was involved in a serious car crash not long before the Blues reached the 2011 FA Cup final and Zaba flew back to Argentina to be by his bedside. He returned in time for the final and came on as an 88th-minute sub for Carlos Tevez as City ended their 35-year wait for silverware with a 1-0 win over Tony Pulis's Stoke City.

Zaba shared right-back duties with Micah Richards during the 2011/12 campaign, but it was his goal that broke the deadlock against QPR as the Blues went on to clinch a dramatic last-day title triumph.

He was voted the MCFC Player of the Year for 2012/13 and captained the Blues several times during Kompany's absence with injury. The only downside of his time with the Club was the 84th-minute red card in the 2013 FA Cup final that City lost 1-0 to Wigan Athletic in added time.

At the end of the campaign, he was also voted into the PFA Team of the Year – the only City player to be nominated by fellow professionals that year. He would add another Premier League title in 2014 as well as a League Cup victory over Sunderland in his best season yet in terms of silverware, and made 48 appearances in all competitions.

For the first time in his City career, injuries inevitably took their toll in 2015/16 and he made just 22 appearances but, for a player who had shed more blood than most in the club's history and made so many bone-crunching challenges, it was hardly surprising.

In 2016/17, he still clocked up 32 appearances before finally ending his stay with the Blues to join West Ham. By then, he'd made 333 appearances all told, scored 12 goals and had countless head stitches and broken noses – courage recognized in a rousing sending-off from the City fans after his final game against West Brom and each time he returns to the Etihad.

ZABALETA, PABLO
2008–17
APPEARANCES
333
GOALS
12
POSITION
Right-back
BORN
Buenos Aires, Argentina

Below: Pablo Zabaleta is all smiles after scoring for City against his future team West Ham at the City of Manchester Stadium in May 2011.

Right: City's legendary warrior celebrates another goal, this one against Watford in 2016.

YAYA TOURÉ

Of all the players who joined City since the club's takeover in 2008, few would argue that Yaya Touré didn't have the most impact. The tall Ivorian played such an integral part in all of the Blues' successes during his time at the Etihad that it is almost impossible to think of a key moment without thinking of Yaya.

Signed from Barcelona in 2010, Yaya was already a Champions League winner with plenty of experience. A powerful, athletic presence, he quickly became synonymous with City's swashbuckling attacking style as he settled in, and it was no coincidence that the Blues ended a 35-year wait for silverware in his first season in sky-blue. It was Yaya's winner in the FA Cup semi-final at Wembley against Manchester United that earned City a place in the final against Stoke, and it was Yaya's winner in the final that finally brought a trophy back to the Etihad in 2011.

But he had only just started.

He was an automatic choice for Roberto Mancini and, throughout the 2011/12 campaign, Yaya was at his inspirational best. When City needed a game-changer, Yaya would inevitably come up with the goods and, as the Blues went head-to-head with United for the 2011/12 title, Yaya's late double strike in the third-to-last game away to Newcastle put City within one win of the title.

Ironically, Yaya limped off in the final-day clash with QPR, but he had already more played his part in the title triumph that followed. His 42 games and nine goals would be exactly matched in 2012/13, but when new manager Manuel Pellegrini arrived, Yaya had his most effective season yet.

Perhaps encouraged to get forward into the box more, shoot and take dead-ball situations, Yaya was magnificent as he scored 24 goals in 49 games and City landed a second Premier League title in three years. And it was his wonder-strike at Wembley against Sunderland that drew City level and on the way to a League Cup triumph. No wonder, in a season when six or seven could have easily won, it was Yaya who was voted the Manchester City Player of the Year.

His influence would continue. He bagged 12 goals in 37 starts during 2014/15 and, in 2015/16, he coolly slotted home the winning penalty in the Capital One Cup final penalty shoot-out with Liverpool.

Yaya's outspoken agent publicly complained when Yaya was left out of Pep Guardiola's Champions League squad, leading the Ivorian being dropped until an apology was received. When it was, he was recalled to the team away to Crystal Palace and scored twice to announce his return. He was less vital to the style Pep liked his teams to play and, although he would add a third Premier League-title medal to his extensive collection, he played just 17 games in all competitions.

A wonderful player, he was a genuine tour de force behind City's many successes from 2010 on.

TOURÉ, YAYA
2010–18
APPEARANCES
316
GOALS
79
POSITION
Midfielder
BORN
Bouake, Ivory Coast

Opposite: Yaya Touré curls in another spectacular free-kick.

Left: After his 316th and final appearance for City, Yaya said farewell to the City fans. He was joined by brother Kolo.

JOE HART

When Joe Hart signed for Burnley on a permanent deal in 2018, it brought an end to his remarkable 12-year association with Manchester City.

Hart followed in the great tradition of iconic Manchester City goalkeepers that included Frank Swift, Bert Trautmann and Joe Corrigan, writing his name into the history books as the most decorated and capped keeper City had ever had.

He joined City in 2006 from Shrewsbury for a fee of just £600,000 after catching the eye of then-goalkeeping coach Tim Flowers. A Shrewsbury lad, Hart made 58 starts for his hometown club over a three-year period. He moved to City having already established himself as the England Under-19s' first-choice goalkeeper and made his City debut against Sheffield United, aged only 19, keeping a clean sheet in a 0-0 draw with the Blades.

That same season, he would spend month-long loans with Blackpool and Tranmere, before returning to City to challenge Andreas Isaksson and Kasper Schmeichel for the last line of defence at Eastlands. He won his first full England cap in June 2008 – a 2-0 win over Trinidad & Tobago – and, very soon had established himself as the nation's No. 1.

When Shay Given was given the City gloves after signing in early 2009, Hart was loaned to Birmingham City for the 2009/10 season. It proved a hugely successful spell, as he was voted the BCFC player of the year, as well as winning himself a place in the PFA Team of the Year.

New City manager Roberto Mancini was keen for Hart to return as his No. 1 for the 2010/11 campaign – the Italian had taken over in the previous December – but the rules of the loan deal meant he couldn't recall Joe earlier than agreed, even though there was a keeper crisis for the final weeks of the season.

Hart's eventual return at the start of the 2011/12 season saw him make a stunning goalkeeping display as he single-handedly kept Spurs out at White Hart Lane with a series of breath-taking saves. He remained as City's keeper for the remainder of the campaign, playing a huge role in the Blues securing Champions League qualification for the first time and, of course, winning the FA Cup to end a 35-year wait for silverware.

The following season, Hart was a commanding presence as the Blues landed a top-flight title for the first time in 44 years – and Joe's celebration with Gael Clichy at the end of the dramatic 3-2 win over QPR on the final day encapsulated a magical moment for the players and supporters.

A huge crowd favourite, Joe went on to win a second Premier League in 2013/14 under Manuel Pellegrini's reign and would also win two League Cups, in 2014 and 2016.

He won four Golden Glove awards for the most Premier League clean sheets with City, and his last official game for the Blues was in 2016 – another clean sheet, against Steaua Bucharest, in a Champions League qualifying match at the Etihad where, fittingly, he wore the captain's armband.

Joe then joined Torino on a season-long loan and would spend the 2017/18 campaign on loan with West Ham United before eventually signing for Burnley on a permanent deal.

Few will forget his many man-of-the-match displays, but his performances against Spurs in 2011, Borussia Dortmund in 2012 and away at Barcelona in 2015 (when it seemed like Lionel Messi v. Joe) almost defied belief.

Capped 75 times by England and with 348 appearances for City, Hart will rightly be remembered as a true Manchester City great, a wonderful professional and a fantastic servant for the Club.

HART, JOE
2006–18

APPEARANCES
348

GOALS
0

POSITION
Goalkeeper

BORN
Shrewsbury

Right: Joe Hart's place in the history of Manchester City is assured as one of the Club's all-time great goalkeepers.

2013-2019: SUCCESS BREEDS SUCCESS

7

7. 2013–2019: SUCCESS BREEDS SUCCESS

Former Real Madrid and Malaga boss Manuel Pellegrini replaced Roberto Mancini, and the Chilean opted to bring a few familiar faces with him to strengthen the Blues ahead of the 2013/14 season. Jesús Navas, Álvaro Negredo and Martín Demichelis arrived from La Liga, while Fernandinho was signed from Shakhtar Donetsk. Carlos Tevez ended his stay with City by joining Juventus.

Previous pages: Leroy Sané fires a low shot past the attempted block by Trent Alexander-Arnold to give City a winning 2-1 lead over Liverpool at the Etihad in January 2019. The Blues would win the Premier League title by one point from the Reds.

Left: Aymeric Laporte (14) is mobbed by team-mates after scoring the goal that gave City a 2-1 lead at the Amex Stadium in Brighton. The Blues won 4-1 and claimed a second consecutive Premier League title.

The new manager knew he had a tough task ahead of him and many supporters were still disappointed that Mancini had gone, but perhaps Mancini's failings in Europe – where Pellegrini had taken unfashionable Villarreal to the semi-final of the Champions League and later guided Malaga to the quarter-final – meant that the change had been justified.

City began the season with a scintillating 4-0 win over Newcastle United, but then lost 3-2 to newly promoted Cardiff. Though the start of the campaign had been far from perfect, Pellegrini earned himself plenty of credit points when the Blues thrashed United 4-1 at the Etihad. Some of the football City were playing was a delight, but they were far from the finished article.

A sobering 3-1 home defeat to Pep Guardiola's Bayern Munich in the Champions League, and three defeats in six Premier League games, suggested the Blues were unlikely to win any silverware at all, but when City did click, they invariably blew teams away.

Negredo was scoring freely, Fernandinho was looking a class act in midfield and some of the team's performances were nothing short of sensational. City beat Norwich 7-0, Spurs 6-0 and Arsenal 6-3, with the brand of beautiful football exactly what the new owners had envisaged their team playing. From late November to the end of

January, the Blues won 12 and drew once in a 13-match Premier League run, scoring 40 goals.

Pellegrini had also guided City through the Champions League group stage for the first time, winning five of the six games, as well as reaching the League Cup final. Liverpool were proving worthy adversaries in the battle for the title, but a 4-1 aggregate defeat to Barcelona ended European hopes.

City won the League Cup at the start of March for the first time in 38 years with a 3-1 win over Sunderland. The Blues had to come from behind to win, with second-half goals from Yaya Touré, Samir Nasri and Jesús Navas completing the victory as Pellegrini won his first trophy.

Bogey team Wigan ended hopes of an FA Cup double with a shock 2-1 win at the Etihad, but in the Premier League, things had been going well until late March, when a stutter in form allowed Liverpool to take the initiative as City dropped two points at Arsenal and then lost a crucial game at Anfield to fall seven points behind the Reds, but they still had two games in hand. However, one of them, a home fixture with bottom club Sunderland, needed a last-gasp Samir Nasri goal to rescue a point in a disappointing 2-2 draw. It looked like a mortal blow to City's title bid.

There were just five games to go and Liverpool were six points clear. Successive wins over West Brom, Crystal Palace and Everton, and Liverpool's 2-0 home defeat to Chelsea, turned the title race on its head – and kept the Londoners in with a shout of becoming champions themselves. The Blues had a much better goal difference and two home games to finish the campaign against Aston Villa and West Ham, and Liverpool's nerves seemed to be getting the better of them as they looked to end a long run without a top-flight title.

The Merseysiders played one of their two remaining games first, away to Crystal Palace,

Above: The prolific Sergio Agüero celebrates being on target again against Tottenham Hotspur at the Etihad.

Right: Edin Dzeko has just scored one of his two goals against Everton in the crucial 3-2 victory at Goodison Park late in the 2013/14 title run-in.

and were cruising 3-0 with only 11 minutes remaining – but, astonishingly, conceded three goals to see the game end 3-3. City effectively needed just four points to all-but guarantee a second title in three years.

Aston Villa arrived at the Etihad having just avoided relegation, but on a rain-swept, tense night at the Etihad, the score remained 0-0 with more than an hour played. Nails were bitten as City fans wondered if a goal would ever come – but, of course, it did, with Edin Džeko opening the floodgates in the 64th minute and City going on to win 4-0. With a goal difference that was 13 better than Liverpool, and with Chelsea now out of the equation, a win on the final day at home to West Ham would seal the title.

This time, there would be no last-day dramas, as a goal in each half from Nasri and Vincent Kompany gave City a 2-0 win and ensured the Blues pipped Liverpool to the title by two points after another thrilling title race had seen City come from a seemingly hopeless situation to chase down their title rivals.

Pellegrini had won two trophies in his first campaign at the Etihad – only the second City boss to ever achieve the feat after Joe Mercer. Not a bad first season!

The Chilean never managed to again reach the heights of his first season as City manager, with his second ending without any silverware. The campaign began with a demoralizing 3-0 Community Shield defeat to Arsenal at Wembley and stuttered along thereafter. Following a 3-1 win at West Brom on Boxing Day, the Blues were very much in the hunt for the title, just three points behind José Mourinho's Chelsea and seven clear of third-placed Manchester United. Frustrating defeats

to Stoke and West Ham, plus dropped points against lowly QPR, had suggested the Blues hadn't kicked on from the previous campaign.

City were out of the League Cup and had just about scraped through to the Champions League group stage, where Barcelona once again awaited in the round of 16. Then, going into the New Year, City dropped 11 points from a possible 18, allowing Chelsea to race seven points clear – a lead they would not surrender.

A disappointing exit to Middlesbrough in the FA Cup and Champions League exit to Barcelona was compounded by a run of four losses in six Premier League games. City at least ended the season with six wins on the bounce and secured runners-up spot, but the season felt like a damp squib in comparison to the previous campaign.

Pellegrini's third season at the Etihad would also be his last. Some excellent business in the transfer market saw Kevin De Bruyne, Nicolás Otamendi and Raheem Sterling all arrive, and City made a superb start to the 2015/16 season, winning the first five Premier League games without conceding a goal.

But three losses on the bounce – two in the league and an opening Champions League group-stage loss to Juventus suggested all was not as rosy as it seemed, and the manner in which Jürgen Klopp's Liverpool dismantled the Blues at the Etihad during a sobering 4-1 home loss had many wondering whether the popular Pellegrini had taken City as far as he could. A defeat at Arsenal just before Christmas left the Blues six points adrift of surprise leaders Leicester City.

Perhaps the title would again slip through the Blues' hands, but there was still a League Cup semi-final with Everton to look forward to and a

favourable Champions League round of 16 tie with Dynamo Kyiv on the horizon.

Though City ended January just three points behind leaders Leicester and having edged past Everton to reach another League Cup final, it was announced that Pep Guardiola would be replacing Pellegrini at the end of the season. And the Blues mixed fortunes continued in a season of contrasts. Three successive league losses, a League Cup final victory over Liverpool and progression to the Champions League quarter-final – it was both a great season and a disappointing one!

The Premier League seemed to be heading to Leicester, but the Blues had their eyes on an even bigger prize after holding Paris St Germain 2-2 in the French capital and then winning the second leg 1-0. Only the mighty Real Madrid stood between City and the UEFA Champions League final.

City perhaps paid the Spaniards too much respect over the two legs, drawing 0-0 at the Etihad and losing 1-0 in the return. Many fans felt the Blues hadn't thrown caution to the wind, particularly in the closing stages of the second leg when just one goal was needed to knock Madrid out of the competition. It was a slightly deflating end to what had been a magnificent run, and the final Premier League games ended disappointingly, with City only scraping into fourth spot on goal difference.

Pellegrini left to a warm ovation from the City fans who had travelled to his final game in charge at Swansea and the likeable Chilean's reign was finally over. The supporters had made a flag in his honour with the words, "This Charming Man", which summed up the overall feeling of his time as City boss, see by all as dignified and, with three trophies and the best Champions League campaign yet, not without success.

Thoughts then turned to the mouth-watering prospect of the man many considered to be the best manager in the world – Pep Guardiola...

Guardiola's first campaign as City manager would be one of assessment and acclimatizing to life in the Premier League. There were no wholesale squad changes, with Claudio Bravo, Nolito, John Stones, Ilkay Gündoğan and Leroy Sané the main summer signings.

The Catalan boss began coaching the players his style of play from the first training session, with the emphasis on keeping the ball, playing with energy and pressing high. He also wanted to see what the majority of players he had inherited were capable of, but perhaps the most telling decision he made was to replace the popular Joe Hart with Chile captain Bravo. The reason was that he wanted his team to play football from the back and felt Hart wasn't the right man. It was a painful and brave decision, but it was one the manager felt needed to be made.

Pep's first mission was to guide City through the Champions League qualifier against Steaua Bucharest, which was achieved comfortably. With a League Cup win and six successive Premier League victories to start the campaign, the Blues had won their opening nine matches under

Above left: Skipper Vincent Kompany celebrates a City goal in another derby win over United.

Above: Alvaro Negredo celebrates after City's League Cup final triumph against Sunderland in 2014. The Spaniard's goals in the earlier rounds were a big part of the Blues' success in the competition.

Guardiola – the best start ever by a new City manager – but a 3-3 Champions League draw with Celtic heralded a mini-dip in form, with no wins in four.

The players were still learning and the whole campaign would be one of gradual progression.

By the time City lost 4-0 at Everton, hopes of another Premier League title were all but over, with Chelsea and Tottenham gunning for the crown, but the January Goodison Park reverse was, in many ways, a pivotal moment for Guardiola and his team. Aymeric Laporte was signed during the January transfer window as the Catalan continued to shape his squad and, although a thrilling round of 16 pairing with Monaco would see City exit the Champions League, the second half of the season saw the Blues continue to improve and look evermore like a Guardiola team.

Pep wanted more from his players and, by that point, knew the personnel he needed to get his team to the next level. The Blues lost just one of the next

17 Premier League games to secure a thirrd-place finish and reached the semi-final of the FA Cup. There were no trophies for Guardiola in his first season, but the foundations had been laid for the 2017/18 campaign.

City were busy during the close season, with some major signings being secured. Bernardo Silva, Benjamin Mendy, Kyle Walker, Danilo and Brazilian goalkeeper Ederson all arrived.

Ederson was installed as the new No. 1 and his distribution and calmness in possession were integral to everything the Blues would do in what would be a record-breaking campaign.

Once again, City began the season in scintillating form, winning 19 of the first 20 Premier League games to establish a huge lead at the top. Liverpool were beaten 5-0, Watford 6-0, Crystal Palace 5-0, Stoke 7-2, Swansea 4-0, Spurs 4-1, Bournemouth 4-0... the Blues were blowing teams away playing beautiful football. Those who wondered whether Guardiola could continue the

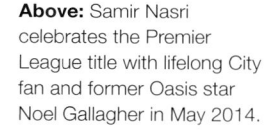

Far left: "This Charming Man": Manuel Pellegrini brought the Premier League title and League Cup to the Blues in his first season.

Left: It's party time as City's 2-0 win over West Ham on the final day of the 2013/14 season secures a second league title in three years.

Above: Samir Nasri celebrates the Premier League title with lifelong City fan and former Oasis star Noel Gallagher in May 2014.

success he enjoyed in Spain and Germany were quickly silenced, as City remained unbeaten in the Premier League until 14 January, when Liverpool edged a 4-3 win at Anfield – but even after that loss, City were still 15 points clear of the chasing pack and cruising toward the Premier League title playing the sort of football that fans had only previously dreamed of.

Progression to the Champions League knock-out stage had been achieved in a canter and, during a 4-2 win away to Napoli, Sergio Agüero scored his 178th goal for City to become the club's all-time leading scorer, overtaking long-time record-scorer Eric Brook's tally of 177.

In February, City won the first trophy of the Pep Guardiola era with a 3-0 League Cup win over Arsenal at Wembley. Goals from Agüero, Vincent Kompany and David Silva completed a comfortable victory for the Blues. Two months later, City were crowned Premier League champions for the third time in seven years, with

a 5-0 victory over Swansea and four games still to play. Goals from David Silva, Raheem Sterling, Kevin De Bruyne, Bernardo Silva and Gabriel Jesús completed the rout. Four days later, City returned to London and beat Arsenal 3-0 in the Premier League. The Blues were unstoppable, but a shock 1-0 defeat to League One side Wigan Athletic in the FA Cup ended hopes of a domestic treble – the third time the "Latics" had ended the Blues' hopes in the competition in five years.

FC Basel were dispatched in the Champions League round of 16 to set up a tie neither City nor Liverpool wanted in the quarter-final. The first leg at Anfield went badly for City, who suffered the heaviest defeat of the campaign as they went down 3-0 to Jürgen Klopp's side. The return leg had seen the Blues ahead inside two minutes, but a legitimate second goal just before the break was ruled offside and, with it, hopes of overturning the deficit. Liverpool won 2-1 on the night and City refocused on securing the title. Four days later,

WITH MANY TOP-FLIGHT AND CLUB RECORDS STILL UP FOR GRABS, THERE WAS NO STEPPING OFF THE GAS FOR CITY, WITH PEP GUARDIOLA DETERMINED THAT HIS TEAM TAKE THEIR CHANCE TO CREATE HISTORY.

City's 3-1 win over Spurs meant the Blues needed just two points to be crowned champions – but a surprise 1-0 win for West Brom over nearest challengers Manchester United meant the title was confirmed without even playing.

With many top-flight and club records still up for grabs, there was no stepping off the gas for City. Guardiola was determined that his team took their opportunity to create history. On the final day of this incredible season, Gabriel Jesús scored the only goal of the game four minutes into added time to beat Southampton and take the Blues to the 100-points mark, and complete a momentous, record-breaking moment. The Blues also scored 106 goals along the way and broke other numerous records, earning the tag "Centurions" for their magnificent achievements.

As hard as it was to top that fantastic campaign, Pep's Manchester City would do exactly that as the Blues embarked on what would be the most successful domestic season in English football history. Algerian playmaker Riyad Mahrez was the only summer arrival, from Leicester City.

The campaign began in August with a 2-0 win over Chelsea in the FA Community Shield at Wembley and a goal in each half for Agüero – the first being his 200th for the club. Yet this would be a season where Liverpool would push City all the way. The champions' Premier League season started almost as impressively as the previous campaign had. The Blues racked up 13 wins and two draws in the first 15 games, scoring plenty of goals and conceding few.

Progress in the League Cup and Champions League was fairly smooth – aside from a 2-1 home loss to Lyon – but Liverpool were matching City stride for stride. So much so that, after a defeat to Chelsea in December, the Blues perhaps felt the pressure, with defeats to Crystal Palace and Leicester City following shortly after. Liverpool continued to win and, by the time the teams met for the first game of 2019, Jürgen Klopp's side were seven points clear. There could be no slip-ups – if the Blues lost to Liverpool, the Merseysiders would open a 10-point gap at the top. City were in no mood to surrender their crown, however, and goals from Sergio Agüero and Leroy Sané helped the Blues to a priceless 2-1 victory and reduced the gap with the leaders to a much more manageable four points. However, there would still be many hurdles to clear in the months that remained.

City's quest for a sweep of domestic silverware continued with the 10-0 aggregate rout of League One Burton Albion in the League Cup semi-final and a 7-0 win over Rotherham United in the FA Cup third round, and Burnley were dispatched 5-0 in the fourth round. The Blues lost 2-1 to Newcastle at the end of January, but Liverpool blew the chance to go eight points clear with a 1-1 draw against Leicester at Anfield the following day. It would be a huge chance missed for Klopp's side.

In February, City landed their second trophy of the season as Guardiola's men beat Chelsea in a tense League Cup final at Wembley to secure the cup for a fourth time in six years. The game ended 0-0 after extra time, with City clinching a fourth trophy in 12 months winning 4-3 on penalties.

A 4-1 win over Newport County also ensured City were still on track to win the FA Cup and, in

the Champions League, a 3-2 win away to Schalke set up a comfortable second leg at the Etihad, which the Blues would win 7-0. The draw for the last eight, however, again pitted City against Premier League opposition, this time in the shape of Tottenham Hotspur.

The FA Cup run continued at Championship side Swansea. The Welsh team scored two first-half goals and led 2-0 after an hour, but Bernardo Silva, an own goal and an Agüero diving header snatched victory from the jaws of defeat and sent City into the semi-final. In the Premier League, the Blues were focused and gradually eating away at Liverpool's lead. It was a fascinating battle, with both teams worthy of the title.

The Blues were back at Wembley to face Brighton in the FA Cup semi-final and an early diving header from Gabriel Jesús was enough to book a place in the final. Now for the Champions League and two epic tussles with Tottenham, the first of which was at the north Londoners' superb new home. City looked to have got off to a dream start when the video assistant referee (VAR) awarded a 13th-minute penalty. But Sergio Agüero saw his effort saved and the hosts went

on to edge the game 1-0. Eight days later, one of the most thrilling games ever witnessed at the Etihad took place. In a game that ebbed and flowed, City went ahead through Raheem Sterling four minutes in, before Spurs responded with two quick goals. Bernardo Silva equalized – all with just 11 breathless minutes played. It was incredible stuff and far from over. Sterling scored again in the 21st minute, but City needed to score again. Just before the hour-mark, Agüero finally put City ahead on aggregate, but two crucial VAR decisions – both of which went against the Blues – were still to come. At the 73-minute mark, a Spurs corner seemed to go in the net via Fernando Llorente's arm but, after numerous replays, the referee awarded the goal. The cruellest twist was still to come. Deep into added time, Agüero raced into the box before passing to Sterling, who slotted the ball home to send the Etihad into a frenzy. Players, staff and supporters celebrated wildly – until the referee indicated that the VAR was checking on a possible offside. Seconds later, it was the Tottenham fans, players and staff going wild as the goal was ruled out. It was agonizing, but there was nothing anyone could do – City were out.

Above: This is my City: Pep Guardiola arrives to take City to the next level.

Top: City fans in their thousands cheer on the team at Wembley during the 2018 League Cup final.

Above: David Silva wheels away after scoring City's third goal against Arsenal in the 2018 League Cup final.

The Blues had to pick themselves up – and quickly – with Spurs again the opposition just a few days later in the Premier League. Phil Foden – a Stockport-born 18-year-old who has come though the club's academy and was very highly rated by manager Guardiola – headed the winner, meaning victory in the penultimate Premier League game of the season against Leicester would put the Blues top. On another night of unbearable tension, the visitors went close a number of times and, with more than two-thirds of the match gone and still no score, it looked as though the epic quest to chase down Liverpool would end on home turf. Then, with no other options open to him, captain Vincent Kompany nudged the ball forward some 30 yards out before unleashing a spectacular shot into the top right-hand corner for a 70th-minute winner that kept City on course for back-to-back Premier League titles. It was also City's 100th goal at home in all competitions during the 2018/19 season – the first time the Blues or any English top-division club had achieved the feat.

Just a few days later, and after an exhausting, relentless campaign, City were crowned Premier

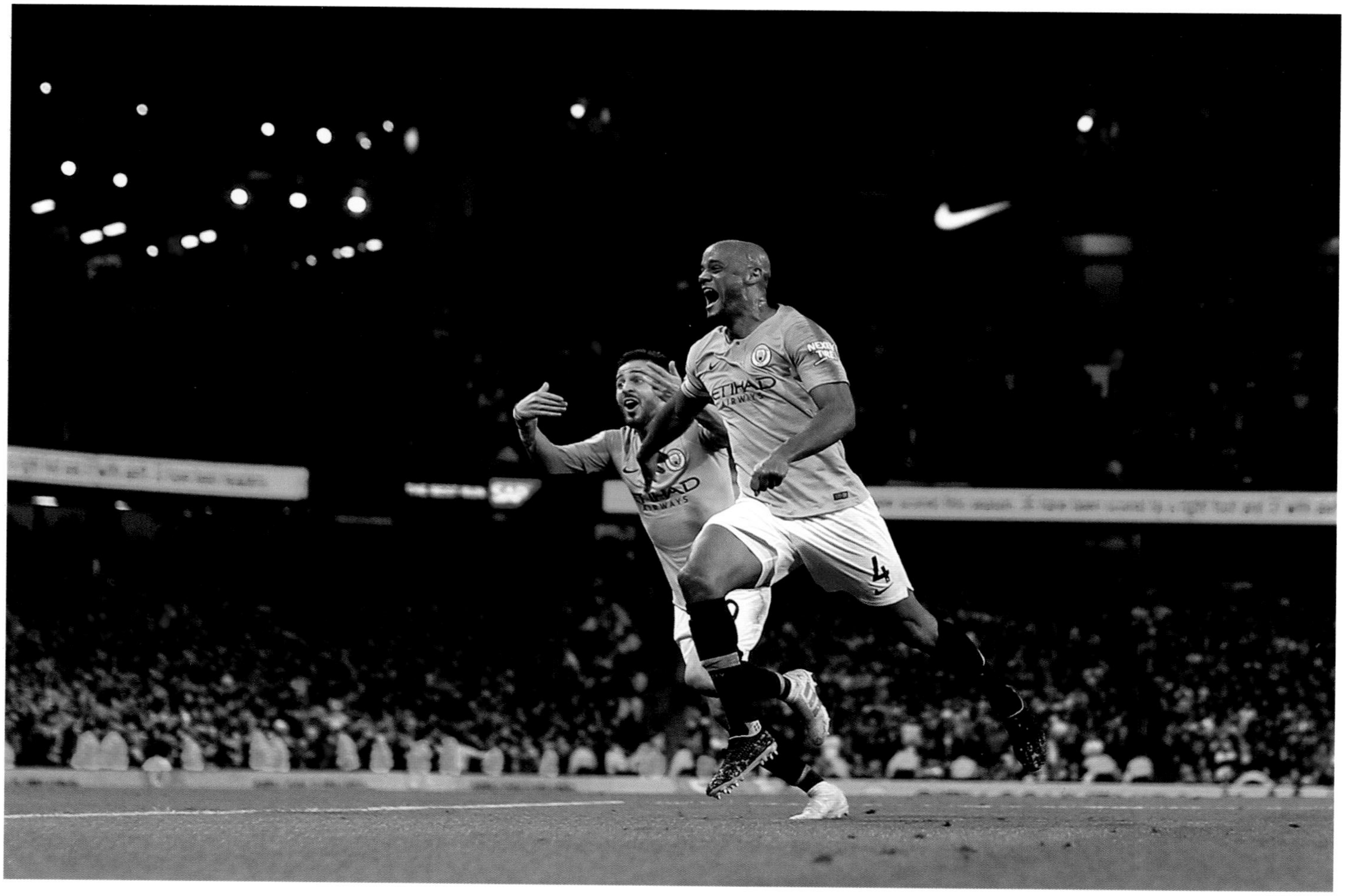

League champions after beating Brighton 4-1 on the final day of the season. Incredibly, it was City's 14th straight Premier League win and saw the Blues end with 98 points – one ahead of Liverpool, who finished with the highest points total for a non title-winning team. It also meant Pep Guardiola's side were the first to successfully defend the title for 10 years. Goals from Sergio Agüero, Aymeric Laporte, Ilkay Gündoğan and Riyad Mahrez saw off the Seagulls at the Amex Stadium.

But this amazing season wasn't quite done yet and City complete an unprecedented quadruple domestic sweep of trophies with a superb FA Cup final win over Watford at Wembley. The Blues thrashed the Hornets 6-0, with goals from David Silva, Gabriel Jesús (2), Kevin De Bruyne and Raheem Sterling (2), to become the first English men's team to win all four domestic trophies – Community Shield, League Cup, Premier League and FA Cup – in one season. It was the perfect end for Pep Guardiola's "Fourmidable" side and a perfect way to lead into the club's 125th anniversary.

It's been quite a journey so far...

Top: Written in the stars – Vincent Kompany's spectacular winner against Leicester puts City on the verge of back-to-back titles.

Above: Another season, another trophy for Sergio Agüero to sip from – this time, it is after City had won the 2019 League Cup.

Top: The Blues celebrate the 2014 League Cup win over Sunderland in the Wembley dressing room.

Above: You beauty! Samir Nasri puts City ahead against Sunderland in the 2014 League Cup final.

Right: Alvaro Negredo has completed a hat-trick in the 6-0 League Cup semi-final first leg win over West Ham.

Left: Pablo Zabaleta savours his and City's second Premier League title win in May 2014.

Above: : Manuel Pellegrini waves goodbye after City's final game of the 2015/16 campaign at Swansea,.

Below: Title parades never get old, as City's 2014 celebrations outside Manchester City Hall prove.

Top left: Combative Brazilian midfielder Fernandinho takes the ball from Real Madrid's James Rodríguez during the 2015-16 Champions League semi-final.

Above: Leroy Sane scores his second goal against nearest Premier League rivals Liverpool to complete a 5-0 win over the Merseysiders in 2017/18.

Left: Kevin De Bruyne scores the winner against Paris St Germain in the Champions League quarter-final second leg at the Etihad in April 2016.

Near right: England right-back Kyle Walker was an important signing from Tottenham Hotspur in 2017.

Far right: The prolific Raheem Sterling has become an integral part of Pep Guardiola's City squad.

Below: Another League Cup success, this one in 2018 after Arsenal had been beaten 3-0 at Wembley.

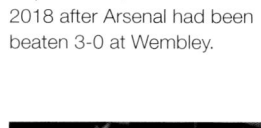

Above: Gabriel Jesus celebrates his last-minute winner against Southampton, ensuring City end 2017/18 as Premier League "Centurions".

Right: The brilliant Brazilian Ederson who has helped to change the way that goalkeepers play all around the world.

Top left: Raheem Sterling's emphatic penalty settles the 2019 League Cup final penalty shoot-out against Chelsea.

Middle left: City players run to celebrate the League Cup shoot-out win over Chelsea with Raheem Sterling and Ederson at Wembley.

Above: Sergio Agüero hugs the trophy and shows four fingers to denote his and City's fourth League Cup final victory in six seasons.

Left: The champagne and tickertape celebrations are alreadyin full swing at Wembley after City had won the 2019 League Cup.

Above: Leroy Sane's second-half winner against Liverpool proved to be crucial in the 2018/19 Premier League title race.

Right: Thank you skipper! Pep Guardiola congratulates Vincent Kompany after his late winner against Leicester City in May 2019.

Top right: Raheem Sterling scores his second goal in the 6-0 FA Cup final demolition of Watford at Wembley in May 2019.

Middle right: Vincent Kompany holds the trophy aloft as City win the FA Cup for the first time in eight years.

Right: Ilkay Gundogan is congratulated after his free-kick puts City 3-1 up at Brighton on the final day of the season.

Top left: A delighted Pep Guardiola celebrates City's final day Premier League title-clinching defeat of Brighton in May 2019.

Above: Gabriel Jesus (right) is hugged by Bernardo Silva after scoring City's second goal in the 2019 FA Cup final at Wembley.

Left: Champions! Vincent Kompany lifts the Premier League trophy for the fourth time in seven years.

Above: Pep Guardiola gets the "bumps" from his City players after the 2019 Premier League title win.

SERGIO AGÜERO

When Sergio Agüero joined City from Atlético Madrid in the summer of 2011, nobody could have predicted the part he would play in the club's history.

The Argentine's journey to the Etihad began as a teenager for his boyhood club, Independiente, where he burst on the scene as a 15-year-old and went on to play 56 times for them, scoring 23 goals. It was that form that alerted La Liga's numerous South American scouts and Atlético paid €20 million for his services.

Nicknamed "Kun" after a cartoon character, Agüero took a year or so to adjust to life in Spain before he became a huge crowd favourite with the club's fans. Over the next five years, he would play 234 games and score 101 goals before deciding to leave Madrid in 2011.

City had been tracking his progress for some time and moved in quickly, securing his services for a fee in the region of £35 million. Agüero made an immediate impact, coming on as a second-half substitute, scoring two and assisting one, in a brilliant 30-minute cameo against Swansea on his debut.

It set the tone what was to come. Sergio would score 30 goals in his first season with the Blues, with the last of those coming against QPR on the final day of the campaign. City had been 2-1 down with 92 minutes played against QPR – a game where only a win would secure the Premier League title. After Edin Dzeko had made it 2-2, the ball was played to Agüero on the edge of the box and he expertly drifted past one defender before smashing the ball home to bag the club's first league title

in 44 years in the most dramatic circumstances imaginable. It is still widely regarded to be the greatest Premier League moment.

He scored 28 goals in 34 games as City won the Premier League again two years later, despite an injury-hit second half of the campaign, and he continued to score goals as the trophies kept coming. Kun's goal away to Napoli in the Champions League in 2017 took him past Eric Brook's total of 177, the City record which had stood since 1939 – and he achieved it in only 264 appearances.

He went on to have his most prolific campaign yet, with 33 goals in 45 appearances in all competitions, including 20 in 31 in the Premier League and eight in eight in the Champions League, further enhancing his reputation as one of Europe's elite strikers.

In the 2017/18 "Centurions" campaign, he bagged 30 goals in 39 matches, and he began the 2018/19 season by scoring both goals in the FA Community Shield win over Chelsea, taking him past the 200-goal mark for the club.

The key to his success has been his consistency, with the 2018/19 season seeing him reach the 30-goal mark for the fifth time in eight years, an incredible record. Sergio has broken virtually every goal record Manchester City had, setting the bar higher each season, and is regarded as perhaps the greatest striker the Premier League has ever seen.

A phenomenal player, he is, without doubt, one of the greatest strikers City have ever seen, and there is every chance he will continue to break more records in the seasons to come.

AGÜERO, SERGIO
2011–present

APPEARANCES
343*

GOALS
237*

POSITION
Striker

BORN
Buenos Aires, Argentina

*as of 12 September 2019

Right: Sergio Agüero celebrates another goal against in the derby against Manchester United. It was City's second in a 3-1 victory at the Eithad in November 2018.

DAVID SILVA

When David Silva agreed to join City in July 2010, few realized the skilful Spaniard would be pulling the strings for almost a decade with a grace and artistry most supporters had never witnessed before.

While his participation in the 2010 World Cup was minimal, here, he was already world champion, still aged only 24 and willing to take a chance in the Premier League – recognized as the most competitive, physical and fastest league on the planet.

In 2010, City, now under the stewardship of Roberto Mancini, made Silva's capture a priority as the sky-blue rebuilding project began to gather pace. Rather than risk Silva being one of the stars of the 2010 World Cup and being usurped by Barcelona or Real Madrid, the Blues began negotiating with Valencia to secure Silva's services after the 2009/10 campaign ended, and on 30 June 2010, it was announced that an agreement was in place to make the Spaniard a City player after the World Cup for a fee of £24 million.

It would be one of the best deals the club ever made.

Like Yaya Touré, it was no coincidence that City ended a 35-year wait for silverware during his first year with the Blues, with an FA Cup triumph against Stoke completing a superb first campaign that also saw the midfield maestro collect three consecutive Etihad Player of the Month awards between October and December.

The following season, inspired by Silva's magical skills and vision, the Blues ended a 44-year wait for a top-flight title winning it on the final day with that dramatic 3-2 defeat of Queen's Park Rangers.

Silva, by now nicknamed *El Mago* (The Magician) by City fans, completed an amazing 12 months by winning UEFA EURO 2012 with Spain, and was also voted into the PFA Team of the Year and collected the Etihad MCFC Players' Player of the Year award.

More titles followed in 2013/14 as City won the Premier League and League Cup and, in 2016, another League Cup winners' medal was added to his collection. But while his club and country honours are legion, he, bizarrely, would never win the PFA Player of the Year prize – one honour City fans feel he could and should easily have won on at least two occasions, had he been even nominated.

Under the tutelage of Pep Guardiola, Silva continued to shine, taking the captain's armband when Vincent Kompany wasn't playing.

For Spain, he has now won 125 caps, scoring 35 goals, and is undoubtedly one of *La Roja*'s greatest players – quite an accolade. He celebrated his 31st year by winning the 2016/17 Manchester City Player of the Year.

Silva added further Premier League titles in 2017/18 and 2018/19, playing some of his best football yet, before announcing in the summer of 2019 that the 2019/20 campaign would be his last with the club.

When Colin Bell, regraded by so many as City's greatest player, says, "Actually, David Silva is the greatest player to have represented the club," you can't help but agree with him.

SILVA, DAVID
2010–present

APPEARANCES
402*

GOALS
71*

POSITION
Attacking midfielder

BORN
Gran Canaria, Spain

as of 19 September 2019

Opposite: *El Mago* – "The Magician" – a truly magical player for City.

Below: Silva, sported a new look – with a shaven head – for the 2017/18 season.

VINCENT KOMPANY

Many fantastic players have arrived at Manchester City since 2008, at the start what has become a decade of incredible success, but the man who led the team and inspired them when they needed it the most was Vincent Kompany.

The Belgian defender spent an incredible 11 seasons with the club, during which time City and their fans have enjoyed unprecedented success. It was no coincidence and it was a long way from his low-key move to City in August 2008.

Kompany arrived relatively unknown in this country, having previously played for Anderlecht and then Hamburg. The fee was less than £10 million and he signed a week before Sheikh Mansour's takeover of the club making his debut, against West Ham United, just two days later.

Under the guidance of Mark Hughes, he was first used as a holding midfielder, but became a central defender as he played regularly in the Premier League. Kompany was instrumental in City's 2010/11 FA Cup win – the club's first major trophy in 35 years and the catalyst for a period of dominance in the English game. He played 50 times that season and established a reputation as one of the finest centre-halves in English football, earning a place in the PFA Team of the Year and winning City's Player of the Season award.

He replaced Carlos Tevez as captain the following season, a position he would retain until his last game for the club in May 2019 and one he held with distinction. There were numerous moments in a fantastic career with the Blues that stand out, but two in particular were pivotal in two epic title races.

In 2012, with City needing a win in the penultimate game of the season to overtake Manchester United in the title race, it was Kompany's emphatic header that sealed all three points and put City in command of their own destiny, having one time been eight points behind the Reds.

Indeed, five days later, a dramatic 3-2 win over QPR sealed the Premier League title – City's first in 44 years, with Kompany outstanding throughout. He was, by then, already considered to be Europe's most complete central defender.

City won a double in 2014 under coach Manuel Pellegrini, scoring a then-English record 156 goals in all competitions. Kompany was named in the PFA Team of the Year for the third time and made 37 appearances in all competitions. The Blues defeated Sunderland to lift the League Cup and just edged out Liverpool in a tense Premier League title race.

Kompany played in the 2016 League Cup final, when City beat Liverpool on penalties, and he scored the second goal in the Blues' 3-0 defeat of Arsenal in the 2018 League Cup final – and his inspired display in the game earned him the man of the match award.

By that time, a succession of muscle injuries and strains had taken their toll on the powerful Belgian international, who would average 21 games per season in his final four campaigns at the Etihad.

In his final season, when Pep Guardiola needed a player to drag his team over the finish line, he turned to Kompany to get the job done. He played in the crucial run-in of games, demanding, cajoling and leading from the front, and when the Blues needed a goal the most, it was Kompany who, once again, delivered.

With the score 0-0 against Leicester City and 70 minutes played, the captain unleashed a 30-yard screamer that secured three points and put the Blues on the brink of a second consecutive Premier League title. He played 86 minutes of the final-day win over Brighton, which confirmed his fourth Premier League title as a City player, and he also started in the 6-0 FA Cup final win over Watford, lifting his 11th trophy as the Blues skipper and confirming him as the greatest Manchester City captain of all time.

He announced his departure shortly after the FA Cup, but his achievements will be forever etched into the club's history books.

KOMPANY, VINCENT
2008–19

APPEARANCES
360

GOALS
20

POSITION
Central defender

BORN
Brussels, Belgium

Right: Captain Fantastic: City's most successful captain of all time celebrates scoring against Arsenal in the 2018 League Cup final at Wembley.

CLUB HONOURS

MANCHESTER CITY FOOTBALL CLUB HONOURS LIST

First Division/Premier League champions:

1936/37, 1967/68, 2011/12, 2013/14, 2017/18, 2018/19

First Division/Premier League runners-up:

1903/04, 1920/21, 1976/77, 2012/13, 2014/15

Second Division/Championship champions:

1898/99, 1902/03, 1909/10, 1927/28, 1946/47, 1965/66, 2001/02

Second Division/Championship runners -up:

1895/96, 1950/51, 1999/2000

Third Division/League 1 play-off winners:

1998/99

FA Cup winners:

1903/04, 1933/34, 1955/56, 1968/69, 2010/11, 2018/19

FA Cup runners-up:

1922/23, 1932/33, 1954/55, 1980/81, 2012/13

Football League Cup winners:

1969/70, 1975/76, 2013/14, 2015/16, 2017/18, 2018/19

Football League Cup runners-up:

1973/74

FA Community Shield winners:

1937, 1968, 1972, 2012, 2019

FA Community Shield runners-up:

1934/35, 1956/57, 1969/70, 1973/74, 2011/12, 2013/14

European Cup Winners' Cup winners:

1969/70

Full Members Cup runners-up:

1985/86

FA Youth Cup winners:

1985/86, 2007/08

MANCHESTER CITY WOMEN'S FOOTBALL CLUB

FA Women's Super League winners:

2016

FA Women's Cup winners:

2017, 2019

Continental Cup winners:

2014, 2016, 2019

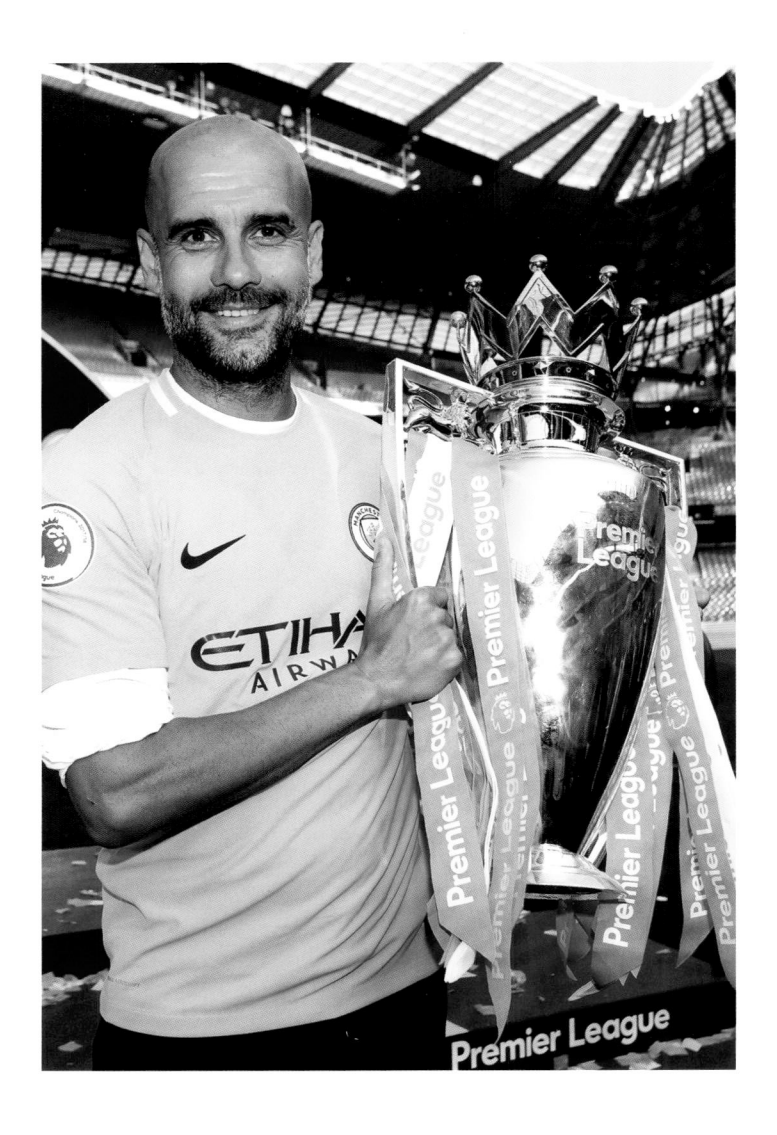

CLUB RECORDS

Record League victory:
11-3 v. Lincoln City (23 March 1895, most goals scored)
10-0 v. Darwen (18 February 1899, widest margin of victory)

Record FA Cup victory:
12-0 v. Liverpool Stanley (4 October 1890)

Record European victory:
7-0 v. Schalke 04, UEFA Champions League round of 16, 2nd leg (12 March 2019)

Highest home attendance:
84,569 v. Stoke City (3 March 1934)

Most League appearances:
561 + 3 sub, Alan Oakes, 1958–76

Most appearances overall:
676 + 4 sub, Alan Oakes, 1958–76

Most goals scored overall:
237*, Sergio Agüero* as of 12 September 2019

Most goals scored in a season:
38, Tommy Johnson 1928–29

Above: Under Pep Guardiola, City have enjoyed astonishing success, winning the Premier League title in consecutive seasons in 2018 and 2019 and sweeping all four domestic competitions in 2019.

INDEX

Numbers in italics refer to the page of captions.
Numbers in bold refer to pages of MCFC Legends.

CREDITS

The publishers would like to thank the following sources for their kind permission to reproduce the pictures in this book. Key: T-top, B-bottom, L-left, R-right, C=centre.

Getty Images: /Burak Akbulut/Anadolu Agency: 170TL; / Gerry Armes/Birmingham Mail/Popperfoto: 4R, 58-59; / Matthew Ashton – AMA: 5L, 112-113; /David Cannon: 91, 96T; /Central Press: 74TL; /Central Press/Hulton Archive: 53; /Ernest Chapman/Mirrorpix: 73; /E Dean/ Topical Press Agency: 27T, 27B; /Adrian Dennis/AFP: 129B; /Denis Doyle: 176TL; /Evening Standard/Hulton Archive: 69; /Fox Photos: 26; /Harry Goodwin/Popperfoto: 97, 102; /Laurence Griffiths: 119L, 126TR, 135; /Keith Hailey/Popperfoto: 68TL; /Richard Heathcote: 127; / Charles Hewitt/Picture Post/Hulton Archive: 46T; /Mike Hewitt: 177BL; /Hulton Archive: 48B; /Keystone-France/ Gamma-Rapho: 12; /Ross Kinnaird: 114, 118, 120-121, 124BL, 124-125, 128T; /Kirby/Topical Press Agency: 18, 30; /Ed Lacy/Popperfoto: 71; /Mark Leech/Offside: 74BR, 92TL, 96BL, 98BR, 103TR, 117R; /Alex Livesey: 105BL, 119TR, 124TC, 132, 176BL; /John Madden/Keystone: 8T; /Jamie McDonald: 126TL; /Edward Miller/Keystone: 34; /Mirrorpix: 41, 63TR, 64, 88, 100-101; /Les Palmer/ Mirrorpix: 65; /PNA Rota: 49C; /Popperfoto: 4BL, 15, 21T, 28, 32-33, 40, 47T, 48T, 55; /Gary M Prior: 116TL, 116TR, 119TL, 123B; /Professional Sport/Popperfoto: 107, 122; /Ben Radford: 126BL, 126BR; /Michael Regan: 189; / Rolls Press/Popperfoto: 63TL, 85; /Bob Thomas: 4BR, 67TL, 67TR, 68TR, 75TL, 76B, 78B, 79, 81, 86-87, 92TR, 93, 96BR, 98L, 99T, 99B, 101TR, 101BR, 103TL, 103BR, 108, 109, 111; /Bob Thomas/Popperfoto: 16L, 21B; /Mark Thompson: 94TR, 104TL; /Hans von der Hardt/ullstein bild: 20T

Manchester City FC: /128B, 140TR, 145TL, 166TL, 172T, 172B, 174BR, 176TR, 177L, 177BR, 185, 187; /Barrington Coombs: 120TL, 148TL; /David Davies: 184; /Mike Egerton: 149BR; /Tom Flathers: 157, 170TR, 173T, 179B, 180TL, 183; /Ed Garvey: 5BL, 136-137, 138, 140TL, 141, 142TL, 142-143, 143TR, 145TR, 146TR, 148TR, 148B, 151T, 151B, 152TL, 152TR, 152B, 153T, 154-155, 156; / Victoria Haydn: 6, 8B, 149T, 158, 159, 171, 175B, 177TL, 178TR, 178L, 178BL, 179T, 180BR; /Sharon Latham: 144, 146TL, 147, 149BL, 150, 153BL, 153BR, 155TR, 155R, 155BR, 161, 166TR, 167TL, 167TR, 168TL, 169TR, 174T, 174BL, 175TL, 175TR; /Matt McNulty: 5BR, 162-163, 164, 173B, 177TR, 178TL, 180TR, 180L, 180R, 181T, 181B; / Tom Yates: 168-169

PA Images: /14TL, 14TR, 16TR, 36, 51, 56, 60, 66TL, 75R, 77, 78T, 82; /Matthew Ashton: 95, 104TR, 104BR; / Barrington Coombs: 124TL; /Gareth Copley: 129T; /Tony Marshall: 130, 131; /Steve Mitchell: 105T, 105BR; /David Rawcliffe: 117TR; /Peter Robinson: 62TR, 66TR; /S&G and Barratts: 19TL, 23R, 24B, 29, 38, 42TL, 45, 49B, 57, 70, 76T; /Neal Simpson: 94TL; /Topham Picturepoint: 44

Shutterstock: /ANL: 4L, 10-11, 39TR, 50TL; /Colorsport: 19TR, 20B, 25T, 25B, 37, 39TL, 42TR, 43, 46B, 47B, 49T, 50TR, 50L, 54, 62TL, 72T, 75BL, 90, 98TR, 104BL, 123T; / Daily Mail: 17, 22-23, 24T, 50BL, 74R; /P Pittilla/Daily Mail: 72B

Every effort has been made to acknowledge correctly and contact the source and/or copyright holder of each picture any unintentional errors or omissions will be corrected in future editions of this book.